Talking It Out

A Guide to Effective Communication and Problem Solving

Joseph M. Strayhorn, Jr.

Research Press Company
2612 North Mattis Avenue   Champaign, Illinois 61821

To my parents

Contents

Acknowledgments

This work was supported in part by NIMH Grant number MH-13112 to the Department of Psychiatry, Duke University Medical Center, through the Sociology and Psychiatry Mental Health Research Program, directed by Jeanne McGee and George Maddox.

I am grateful to my teachers, students, friends, and colleagues at Duke University for supporting and encouraging me in my work on this book and the methods described in it. I especially thank Marilyn Bentov, Keith Brodie, Katherine Buckner, Frederick Hine, Charles Keith, Marguerite Meyers, Charles Schunior, and Adrian Verwoerdt. I also thank Carol Hackett, Rebecca Kyff, Robert Kyff, Donna Neff, and Douglas Neff for their suggestions. I am grateful to my therapy clients for what they have shared with me and taught me.

1 The Principles Behind This Book

Conflict Is Everywhere

I wrote this book for people interested in ways of solving interpersonal problems and conflicts: married couples, people at work, mental health professionals and their clients, people who interact with other people; that is, just about everybody. Whenever people do things together, there will be times when their desires conflict. Conflict is the rule, not the exception, in human relationships. You want to borrow something, I'd rather keep it. You want us to eat at a French restaurant, I prefer Chinese. You want to keep talking, I want to get back to work. You want us to visit your parents, I'd rather stay home. You want me to hurry up, I want you to slow down. Whether or not we must deal with interpersonal conflict is not the issue; how we can best deal with it is the issue.

When we have a conflict of desires, we have several options. We can level with each other and negotiate, or we can avoid the issue and hope that it will go away by itself, or we can attack each other and defend ourselves as vigorously as possible, or we can talk around the issue in such a way that we muddy the waters and leave ourselves so confused that we've forgotten what we were trying to get in the first place!

When we negotiate, we have another choice. We can base our incentives on reward or punishment: we can hold out carrots or sticks. If I let you know that I will call you names and act hostile unless you do what I want, I am basing your incentive on punishment. You might do what I want to avoid punishment. On the other hand, if I let you know that I will be grateful and do some things that you want if you do what I want, I am basing my incentive on reward. Although there are many books and articles about psychological experiments concerning the effects of reward and punishment, you don't have to read them to realize that I like a relationship better if I am anticipating reward rather than avoiding punishment. I tend to stay around people who make me feel good and avoid people who make me feel bad.

Facilitative and Obstructive Messages
In this book I will introduce a language we can use to think and talk about communication. The terms I define will let us specifically and concretely look at what we say and do so that we may more intelligently choose how to communicate according to what works best. I have chosen, from the rich smorgasbord of psychological writings and from my own experience, a number of ways of communicating that pay attention to various *types of messages.*

If you walk into your house and find my junk everywhere and everything is messy, you can send me a message in several ways. You can say, "You are a good-for-nothing slob!" or "If you don't clean up this stuff right now, I'm kicking you out of here!" or you can say nothing and just glare and scowl at me. Or, you can say, "I'd like you to pick up your things, please" or "We have a problem in that when you leave your things around it makes me irritated. Can we think of some options for dealing with this, please?" These and other ways of reacting will be labeled in future pages so that they may be conveniently referred to. Although all the statements in our example are basically expressing dissatisfaction with the messiness, some of them would provoke very different reactions than would others. These reactions can be fairly well predicted from the type of message that is given.

Statements like, "You are a good-for-nothing slob," for example, can be classified as "You Are Bad" statements. Fairly predictably, they produce hurt, angry, or defensive feelings in the listener. On the other hand, "I'd like you to pick up your things, please," is an example of an "I Want" statement. This type of message conveys a wish without eliciting so much hurt, anger, or defensiveness.

I have often seen people (sometimes myself) sincerely trying to solve problems, but using messages that avoid or confuse the issue, attack the other person, and defend oneself. As we grow up, most of us learn communication habits quite unsystematically. We pick up these habits in a helter-skelter manner from parents and peers and by trial and error. Seldom does conscious choice play much of a role. By recognizing, however, different types of messages and how they affect relations between people, we can consciously choose messages according to which effects we wish to produce or avoid.

Although it is impossible to make hard-and-fast rules, I have divided the kinds of messages into two groups, according to whether they are usually *facilitative*—they leave the two people friends—or *obstructive*—they make it more difficult for people to be friends. I don't think of these terms moralistically—as right or wrong—rather, I think in these terms: a message produces a desired effect or a not-so-desired effect in a particular set of circumstances. If someone is about to physically harm me, I probably care very little whether or not we stay friends. I would not hesitate to run away, thus cutting off communication, or to threaten him in order to protect myself. Communication cutoffs and threats are classified as obstructive messages, but that doesn't mean they are never appropriate. I choose among all my options according to what produces the most desired effect.

Nevertheless, in a large percentage of interactions facilitative messages work better than obstructive ones, and the whole thrust of this book will be toward using more facilitative messages and fewer obstructive ones.

The Principle of Habit Strength

Learning to use different kinds of messages to produce more desirable effects cannot be accomplished overnight. Most of us have learned to respond to conflict situations by habit. The strength of habits is great and usually difficult to break. Thus you can't learn better problem-solving techniques in a sudden flash of insight; it takes practice—and more practice. It is like learning to play a musical instrument, not like a religious conversion. Therefore, this book is loaded with exercises, just like a piano instruction book.

If the principle of habit were news to anyone, it would be bad news and good news. The bad news is that it takes work and practice to change communication habits. The good news is that, given work and practice, you can be almost sure of making a beneficial change. There is nothing (or at least not much) mystical or magic or beyond understanding.

The Principle of Fear and the Desensitization of Fears

Habit makes it difficult to change how you communicate. Another barrier is fear. Often when an obstructive message is used, it is used because it is less scary than any other format. For example, when our imaginary person walks into the living room and sees that it is a mess, he may choose to say nothing. But he may harbor silent resentment because he may be afraid to voice his wants or feelings. He may be frightened of the other person's retaliation, or of his own angry impulses, or of violating some rule about being a self-sacrificing person. His silence protects him from his fear.

People use many kinds of obstructive messages to defend themselves against fear. The fear of "losing face" is a particularly common fear.

In the process of giving up obstructive messages for facilitative ones, therefore, there will be some scary moments. Fortunately, however, fears may be gradually overcome, through a process called *desensitization.* When desensitizing a fear, you figure out a hierarchy of situations from least scary to most scary. Then you expose yourself to these situations, moving gradually up the hierarchy, taking time to get used to a not-too-scary situation before exposing yourself to progressively difficult situations. Mastery of one situation will prepare you for the next, so that no one situation will overwhelm you with fear.

Hopefully you will be able to use the various exercises in this book to move from least scary to most scary situations, thus developing the steps of a desensitization hierarchy that fits your needs. Labeling responses can be a rather comfortable academic exercise; fantasy and role-playing exercises may be a good deal more scary; using adaptive messages that relate to real conflicts with real people may be still more scary. Your task is to work at the level or levels at which you accomplish the most and suffer the least.

The Principle of Shaping

The term *shaping* usually refers to the way the trainer or educator or therapist rewards the learner for small increments of improvement. She rewards the small improvements the learner makes on the way to his larger goal and thus directs or "shapes" his development.

Shaping also is a helpful concept when you use it to reward yourself. Self-reward is more subtle than reward actually given by someone else, but it is every bit as real. In this strategy you refuse to put yourself down for being where you are now; instead, you establish a goal, and reward yourself for every little increment of improvement on the way toward that goal. You remind yourself to celebrate. You think, "Hey, I am able to do something I couldn't do before. I am able to do something a little easier than I could before. That's great! I may not be there yet, but I'm moving!" In other words you reward yourself for bits of progress. This is shaping. Notice that shaping does not call for any use of

5

punishment. A statement like, "I should be able to do this already—I'm not—that means I'm worthless—how terrible," is an example of self-punishment. When it is going on strongly, the self-reward process is overshadowed by it. Various studies give evidence that this method doesn't work as well.[1]

The ability to work on the basis of self-reward rather than self-punishment is a habit you can develop. This habit makes learning communication (or anything else) more fun; it also goes hand in hand with learning to use more reward and less punishment in interpersonal relations.

The Principle of Social Exchange and the
Skill of Enjoying Giving

What is the purpose of communication and negotiation, anyway? Some theorists have been able to explain a great deal of what goes on in human relationships by the notion of social exchange. The notion is that people tend to be happy with one another when they can work out an exchange of behaviors, each of which is more rewarding to the other than it is costly to oneself. If I scratch your back, and you scratch mine, and it's rewarding for each of us to get scratched and not very costly for either of us to do the scratching, we both come out ahead on the exchange. The general paradigm is that person A does something kind for person B, and person B does something kind for A in return. One way of viewing the communication process is as a way of working out such exchanges.

But there is something greater than social exchange, something we may call the skill of enjoying giving. Some people have learned to derive pleasure from within when they are able to make someone else happy. With this skill, a new paradigm is possible. Person A does something kind for

---

[1] See the Chapter by M. J. Mahoney, reference 16 in the reference list, for a review of these studies.

Person B. B enjoys the kind act, and A enjoys B's enjoyment. (And B might even enjoy A's enjoyment of B's enjoyment!) Both people feel better, even though there has been no "exchange" in the usual sense.

This second paradigm allows wonderful things to happen. It enables people not to have to keep a mental balance sheet of who owes the other. It enables family members to rise above squabbling and haggling and to move to a climate of cooperation. It enables couples to stay loyal to each other even though one of them can no longer offer the same "rewarding behaviors" to the other because of illness or age or financial disaster. It renders many of the differences between people as nonproblems that do not even need to be talked out. Indeed, this simple sequence may be the most important paradigm for all human relationships: it makes love possible.

It is important to notice that the sequence cannot take place without someone to accept the kind act as well as someone to perform it. The inability to receive can be as big a problem as the inability to enjoy giving, although probably a less common one.

There are times when social exchange is most appropriate (for example, when shopping for a used car or an insurance policy) and other times when the ability to enjoy giving is most appropriate (for example, when caring for an aged parent). Both paradigms have their place.

Now to return to the question for this section: what good are the communication strategies taught by this book? They are useful, if not essential, in both paradigms. If I can avoid antagonizing the other person, make my wishes known, find out the other person's wishes, explore various options, and make decisions accordingly, then I am much better equipped to bring happiness to others and to allow them to bring happiness to me.

2 Strategies in Learning Communication

Ways of Practicing Communication and Problem Solving

As I mentioned in Chapter 1, it takes a lot of practice to improve communication skills. There are four ways that I know of for practicing skill in communication.

The first way is fantasy. You have the power to imagine any scene you wish, one that has happened to you, one that happened to someone else, or one that is purely a product of your creativity. In this fantasied scene you may practice relating in new ways, using messages that are chosen rather than determined by habit. With each imaginary practice session, the desired habit becomes strengthened.

Athletes have used this method of practice successfully: skiing down slopes, shooting foul shots, returning tennis shots, all in the imagination. (For some reports on these methods, see references 25 and 26, by R. M. Suinn.) Fantasy and the imagination may be our most underutilized resources.

There are several exercises in this book in which a scene is set up and a dialogue related. Some of the exercises will ask you to translate from obstructive to facilitative messages; others will ask you to make up a facilitative message before reading the response given in the dialogue. These are all fantasy exercises: when you do them, it will be most helpful if you create the setting in your imagination, make yourself one of the characters, and vividly imagine yourself speaking. This strategy will give you a large amount of productive practice.

Hopefully, the ability may be cultivated through the use of these exercises to do fantasy exercises using the remembered dialogues of your own life. To be able to go back to a remembered scene or forward to an anticipated one and practice responding and handling it in the way you really wish to is an ability that will be extremely useful.

The second way of practicing is role playing. Two or more people set up a scene and play the parts of the characters in it. The actors may play themselves, imaginary people, or other people in their lives. As with fantasy, role playing provides almost limitless opportunities for practice. Rather than talking about a situation, the situation can be brought into the present, into direct experience. By starting with relatively "easy" scenes, that is scenes relatively free of threatening memories or associations, you can pick up negotiating and problem-solving skills in a safe environment. Then you can confront more emotion-charged problems as you acquire the skills necessary to handle them successfully. This is how you can use a desensitization hierarchy, as discussed in Chapter 1. I have listed various structures for role-playing exercises in Chapters 5, 6, 8, 9, and 10 and various situations for role-playing practice in Chapters 5, 6, and 11.

The third way of practicing is through some structured setting in which the norm is open communication and examination of communication and its effects. With this approach people discuss real issues, but the ground rules of the experience give them a certain degree of protection. Group therapy or family or marital therapy or a growth group may be an example of this sort of setting. Or, two or more people may simply set up a regular time to discuss real issues, paying special attention to observing and reshaping the way they communicate.

And finally "the cold, cruel world," or "life" (however you want to look at it) is the final and most ever-present arena for practice in human relationships and problem solving. You can cultivate the ability to keep conscious, at some level, of how you are communicating and to remind yourself to celebrate each bit of progress you make. Also important is the ability to see unfortunate misunderstandings and miscommunications as opportunities for learning and as data on how to make things happen better in the future, not as totally horrible events presenting no opportunity for the extraction of anything valuable.

In Chapters 5, 6, and 11, I list various situations for problem-solving practice. It is helpful to continue this gathering of a conflict list with examples from your own life. If you are doing communication training in a group, you will want to generate situations that are especially relevant to your particular group. For example, a group of co-workers might generate many work-related conflict situations. As you become a connoisseur of conflicts, you may start seeing interpersonal situations as challenging problems—somewhat like puzzles or brain teasers—only more interesting and vital because they involve the emotions as well as the intellect. Gradually they will then be seen as less and less threatening.

Keeping Track of Your Progress
In any course of study, it is of great benefit to be able to monitor your progress as accurately as possible. Accurate record keeping helps provide rewards: you can see progress being made. Also, when you keep accurate records, it is easier to discover what techniques lead to quicker progress than others.

The following are some suggestions for monitoring yourself as you learn communication.
  1. To monitor the kinds of conflicts in your life and how well you handle them, keep a "conflict record." In this record, jot down every day each situation in which your wants did not coincide with those of another, any situation similar to the ones in this book. For each situation,

rate on a scale of 0 to 10 how well you think you handled the situation. You may explain the number by a simple jotted explanation of what you did—for example, "0—I blew up, then stomped off." Or, "6—I negotiated; would have liked to have stuck up for myself more." If possible, keep this record for a baseline period of time prior to the communication course you teach yourself. Then see how the satisfaction level changes as you work on solving problems more effectively. As I implied in the introduction, the goal is not a conflict-free life—that is impossible without living the life of a hermit. The goal is satisfactory handling of the conflicts of wants that are bound to come up.

2. An inexpensive tape recorder is a valuable piece of material in learning interpersonal problem solving. Here is one way to use it. You and your partner agree to sit down together at regular intervals and discuss one problem. Tape record the first three or four minutes of each discussion. (Most people tire of listening to the tape if it is much longer than this. Plus, the time limit helps get you into the habit of moving quickly to the point of the problem.) When you sit down the next time, start recording where you left off. As you progress, you will be able to hear the progression in your communication styles. You will also find it valuable to pick out the types of messages you want to use less often, or more often, and count them in the recorded segments. More ambitious procedures can be devised; however, I think it is always best to keep in mind beforehand that record keeping can be tedious and that the least tedious procedure you can come up with will be most likely to last the longest.

3. If you are learning communication in a larger group, one very effective procedure is to divide into groups of threes. Two people negotiate a role-play situation, and the third observes and monitors the interaction. The

observer keeps a tally of the obstructive and facilitative messages used by each partner for a standard length of time (around two minutes is enough). During the rest of the interaction, she jots down examples of various responses and messages that each sent. At the end of the interaction, she feeds back this information to the two. The two may then categorize their messages, feel good about the ones they liked, and mentally rehearse a replacement for the ones they didn't like. They may compare their tally of responses to those of previous interactions. And, finally, the observer may make other comments and raise questions about the general style of the interaction. The observer will probably do well to stay out of discussing issues concerning the content of the problem and to confine her remarks to the types of messages, that is, the process of the discussion.

When keeping track of your progress, it is important to rely on self-reward for progress and to deemphasize self-punishment for behaviors needing improvement. That is, when recalling an instance of using a communication format that was desirable and helpful, I suggest saying to yourself, "Hooray for me!" But in recalling an instance in which the communication format was undesirable and unhelpful, I would not say, "Boo for me—I am a bad person—I'll never learn—I'm neurotic" or similar self-punishing statements. Rather, I would say, "I would rather have done it differently than I did it. I'll practice in my mind doing it differently, and not punish myself for being imperfect. It's OK to be imperfect."

Hooray for you in getting this far in this book!

3 Facilitative Messages

With all due fanfare, then, let's begin the naming and description of types of messages that I previewed in Chapter 1. Because it's hard to stop using an obstructive message without first having a facilitative message to replace it, I'll start with facilitative messages.

1. I Want Statements

Definition: This is a statement of the type "I want you to do *this*," where *this* is a specific behavior. ("I'd like you to do this," "Would you do this," "How about doing this," etc., are also included under this category.)

Examples: "I want you to tell me how you feel, but I don't want you to yell at me and call me names."

"I want you to let me work by myself on this project for a while, and then I'll get together with you and report to you on it."

"I want us not to go visit your mother next Sunday, but to spend the time by ourselves."

"I'd like you to pick up these things that you've left around the house, if you don't mind."

"I'd like it if you would stop being sarcastic with me."

"I don't want to argue with you about my parents until

we finish discussing this issue that applies to the two of us."

Effects: Satisfaction, by definition, is a state of getting what one wants; many of these wants can be satisfied only by other people. Mutual meeting of wants is the goal of relationships, and the I Want statement is the simplest route to that goal.

Use of the I Want statement encourages me to formulate in my own mind what I really want. This task is a bigger undertaking than it seems for most of us. We are very capable of feeling vague dissatisfaction with the way things are without imagining what we want in their place.

Even when we know what we want, customs and inhibitions often make it difficult for us to ask directly for what we want. The state of not getting what we want and being afraid to ask for it is very unpleasant. When I give you an I Want statement, you are given the information necessary to know how to meet my wants if you choose to do so. If you do, that's great! If you don't, at least I'm relieved of the conflict of wanting and being afraid to ask. And after repeated I Want statements, if you still don't meet my want, I now know that it's time to think about getting it met in some other way, or learning to get along without it. With I Want statements, I'm trying to get what I want in as direct and straightforward a manner as possible, one that is conducive to negotiation instead of nonproductive hostility.

2a. I Feel Statements

Definition: This is a statement of the form, "When you did *that thing*, I felt *this way*." *That thing* is a behavior that the other person did, and *this way* is a specific feeling that you have had.

Examples: "When you were talking so loud and slapping

people on the back, I felt embarrassed."

"When you put your hand on my shoulder, just after I'd sat down, I really felt good."

"I felt irritated just then when you told me to clean the place up."

"When you caught my eye from across the room and winked at me, I felt really close to you."

Note that in these examples there is a "feeling word" in each sentence, a word that names an emotion: *embarrassed, good, irritated, close*. A statement like, "I feel that you didn't spend enough time with the children," is *not* an I Feel statement as I am defining it! What the speaker is really saying is, "I *think* that you don't spend enough time with the children." If, on the other hand, the speaker said, "When I think of how little time you spend with the children, I feel sad," this is an I Feel statement. It contains a feeling word, namely *sad*.

Effects: When I make an I Feel statement to you, I have to get in touch with my own feelings. It gives you information about me and my feelings and allows you to adjust your behavior accordingly.

It allows a message undistorted by assumptions but which reports on perceptions. For example, "You are a slob," carries assumptions about a person who has not been neat; there is implication that the lack of neatness pervades his whole character and that the speaker rejects him as a person. On the other hand, the I Feel message, "When you leave things around the house, I feel irritated," is a much clearer communication. The speaker is reporting on his external perception of things around the house and his internal perception of being irritated. These give information to the other person without attacking his self-esteem.

17

Definition: These are special cases of I Feel statements. They take the format, "I liked it when you did *that thing*," or, "I didn't like it when you did *that thing*." *That thing* is a specific behavior.

Examples: "I liked it when you were able to tell me what I was doing that was bothering you."

"I didn't like it when you were yelling at me and calling me names."

"I liked it when I saw you loosen up and have a good time playing with our daughter."

"I don't like it when you blow smoke in my face like that."

Effects: Pleasure and displeasure are perhaps the most basic of feelings. The use of these I Like and I Don't Like statements allows you to tell the other what gives you pleasure and displeasure. Thus both of you can find out how to make each other happier.

The I Don't Like statement can be very useful as a catharsis: that is, it allows you to get off your chest some gripes that otherwise would remain as silent resentment. However, researchers, teachers, and therapists have found that reward is more beneficial than punishment in changing behavior in the long run. It will be helpful if you follow an I Don't Like statement with I Like statements later on if the other person does make any change in the desired direction. If you have already noticed any movement in the desired direction at all, an I Like will probably encourage the other person to change more than an I Don't Like. For example, "I like it when you stand up straight like you're doing now" will probably be more effective than, "I don't like it when you slouch around like you do most of the time."

Definition: A Reflection is telling the other person what you have perceived or heard or imagined to be going on in his mind, so that he may confirm or deny your impression. In your own words, you say back to him the message you got, in order to check it out. (This type of message has also been called active listening, checking out, and paraphrasing.)

Examples: "Sounds like that really upset you."

"Are you saying that you'd like me to be less controlling?"

"Do you mean you'd like me to leave you alone for a while?"

"What I'm hearing you say is that my not consulting you on this before I did it caused you a lot of embarrassment, right?"

"I have a fantasy that you didn't like my giving you advice like I just did. Is that right?"

"In other words, the issue of cleaning up the house is not so important to you as whether I care about you, and when I wouldn't do it for you, you took it as a sign that I didn't care?"

Effects: The addition of this type of message to either of the two partners' repertoires can by itself make tremendous improvements in the communication and conflict-resolution process. Why is it so helpful?

First, it encourages each person to really listen to the other. Rather than rehearsing in my mind the next thing I am going to say as I wait for you to finish talking, I must really listen if I am to make an accurate Reflection. If I haven't listened, I'll learn about it when you answer "no" to my Reflection. If I get a "no," I try again, listening harder this time. If I get a "yes," I pat myself on the back for hearing and understanding your message.

Second, the Reflection process lets you know your message was received. That is, not only am I more likely to get the message, but also you know when I've gotten it. This usually makes you feel better about the communication process.

Third, the Reflection process keeps distorted messages from being received. There are two places where distortion can occur: you can do an inadequate job of translating your internal mental state into words and gestures, or I can do an inadequate job of translating your words or gestures into an internal mental state. If distortion comes up at either of these points, a "no" will be your reply to my Reflection. Then we can discard that distorted message and try again to express and hear it better.

Fourth, in heated discussions the Reflection process tends to slow down the interchange and to allow us time to think, to reason, rather than simply to respond in a reflex manner without thinking.

Fifth, a Reflection spoken in a calm, accepting tone of voice gives two messages: not only "I hear you saying this," but also, "It is OK to be thinking or feeling these things; these can be dealt with; these are not horrible, though they might be unpleasant." Hearing a very scary aspect of oneself reflected in an unafraid manner helps in the process of acceptance of self and desensitization of fears of various aspects of the self.

The word *fantasy* is useful in making reflections when the communication from the other person was only a hint or a suggestion. It allows the reflector clearly to label the idea as tentative, as something to be confirmed or disconfirmed by the other.

3b.   Reflection of Feelings

Definition: A special type of reflection in which a "feeling word" such as *angry, sad, scared, happy, relieved*, etc., is used to describe your perception of the other person's state.

Examples: "Sounds like that made you really happy, but you feel guilty about it making you happy. Is that right?"

"I'll bet you felt relieved when that happened, huh?"

"You're really angry at me!"

Effects: Feelings are basic. In the communication process it often is useful to get beyond the complexities of ideas and the convolutions of theories about what is going on to the feelings the other person is having. Reflections of feelings do all that other reflections do, with this extra added attraction!

4. The Open-Ended Question

Definition: The Open-Ended Question specifies the general area of interest but lets the specific content of the answer be decided upon by the person answering the question.

Examples: "I'm interested in hearing something about how you feel our project is going."

"Tell me about your reactions to the new system."

"What's your job like?"

"What kind of things happened to you today?"

"What are your thoughts about the way I acted at supper?"

"What have you been up to?"

"Wow, tell me some more about that!"

Effects: When you offer an Open-Ended Question, you are offering your attention and interest in whatever I choose to make as a reply. By asking a nonspecific question, you are encouraging me to come up with whatever is most important to me. Open-Ended Questions are especially useful to people who are dissatisfied with the fact that they "just don't talk to each other." Open-Ended Questions are useful in starting off communication, and are most effective when accompanied by Reflections and other messages that encourage communication to continue.

5. The Direct Question

Definition: A Direct Question asks for a specific bit of information.

Examples: "How long did your trip last?"
"Who is your boss?"
"Have you been having an affair with another woman?"
"What was it that happened that upset you?"

Effects: When you need to find out a specific piece of information, the Direct Question allows you to do it efficiently.

Exercise 1
Labeling Facilitative Messages

Each of the following statements is an example of one of these types:

I Want statement
I Feel statement
I Like, or I Don't Like statement
Reflection
Open-Ended Question
Direct Question

Identify each of the following statements as an example of one of the above categories. Answers, if you need them, are at the end of the exercise.

Situation: Jane, the boss, and Sally, the secretary, are talking.

1. Jane says, "Sally, I'm interested in hearing your reactions to the job so far. How has it been going for you?"
2. Sally replies, "When you ask that, I feel a little uneasy."
3. She continues, "I don't want you to get upset if I'm too frank with you."
4. Jane replies, "You're concerned that if you talk openly with me you might stand to lose out?"
   Sally nods "Yes."
5. Jane replies, "I like it when people I work with let me know exactly what's on their minds."
6. Jane continues, "I want you to let me know what's on your mind and to realize that your job and raises, and so forth, depend on how well you work, not how much you praise me."
7. Sally replies, "That makes me feel good to hear you say that."
8. Sally continues, "Well, some of the things you ask me to do, they just bug me."
9. Jane replies, "Humh! Tell me about these things."
10. Sally replies, "Well, like when you ask me to do things like exchange your husband's shirt at the store, or to get theater tickets for you, or reserve tennis courts. That kind of thing just irritates me."
11. Jane replies, "You don't like doing the things that are personal matters for me and that don't have any connection to the business per se?"
12. Sally replies, "That's right. I just feel kind of put upon doing stuff like that. It's not what I was hired to do, and it bothers me."
13. Jane replies, "I'm glad you told me how you feel about these things."
14. Jane continues, "I still want you or someone else to occasionally do these things for me because it does free

up time for me for other things, and I want that very much."

15. Jane continues, "Do you have any solutions in mind at this moment?"

16. Sally thinks and says, "I want to do what you need done—it just bothers me, though."

17. Jane replies, "I want to think about this some, and I'd like you to do that, too, and I want us to see what we can figure out about it after we've thought about it for a day or two."

18. Sally says, "I'd like for us to do that too."

19. Jane replies, "What else has been on your mind lately—what other reactions do you have to the job situation?"

Answers to Exercise 1

1. Open-Ended Question
2. I Feel statement
3. I Want statement
4. Reflection
5. I Like statement
6. I Want statement
7. I Feel statement
8. I Feel statement
9. Open-Ended Question
10. I Feel statement
11. Reflection
12. I Feel statement
13. I Feel statement
14. I Want statement
15. Direct Question
16. I Want and I Feel statements
17. I Want statement
18. I Want statement
19. Open-Ended Question

Exercise 2
Making up Facilitative Messages

Make up three or four examples of each of the following facilitative messages, and imagine yourself saying them to someone. Which are currently "in your repertoire," and which feel more new to you?

I Want statement
I Feel statement
I Like and I Don't Like statements
Reflections
Open-Ended Question
Direct Question

We now continue with facilitative messages.

6. *Agreeing with Part of a Criticism or Argument*

Definition: Agreeing with Part of a Criticism or Argument is used to respond to a criticism or argument or challenge or resistance by refusing to argue with it and by agreeing or sympathizing with some portion of it. The extent of agreement can be as little as acknowledging the remote possibility that there may be some truth to the argument or as much as heartily agreeing and going even further than the critic went.

Examples: John has just said to Mary, "You don't have any sense!" Mary replies, "It's true that I could be smarter than I am." She agrees with some portion of the criticism and avoids getting hooked into a discussion of whether she has sense or not.

Peggy has asked Ralph to turn the music down. Ralph has replied, "You call that music loud? That isn't loud at all." Peggy replies, "It may not be all that loud, but I still want it turned down." By saying, "It may not be all that loud," Peggy agrees with the possibility of some truth in Ralph's argument, thus avoiding getting hooked into a discussion of whether the music is loud or not.

Jean has asked Alex where he has been going at night when he goes out. Alex has replied, "You're paranoid to ask something like that!" Jean replies, "Maybe it is paranoid of me, but I still want to know where you've been going at night." She agrees with the possible truth of the criticism in order to avoid hassling over whether she is paranoid or not.

Effects: Agreeing with Part of a Criticism or Argument is used partly to avoid wasting time arguing over matters that will get neither person anywhere. In the second example above, Peggy knows that she and Ralph could argue forever over whether the music is "loud" and never settle anything. She knows that she has the right to ask that it be turned down whether it is "loud" or not. This want of hers is the real issue, not some abstract notion of how loud something has to be to be loud.

Another effect of Agreeing with Part of a Criticism or Argument is that it enables you to get into the habit of thinking, "I don't have to be perfect. I have the right to ask for what I want even if there is some truth in the criticisms I am hearing. I don't need to defend myself against every attack. I can still be basically OK even with some faults." This way of thinking is a very great aid to communication and negotiation since very many communications get fouled up when people waste time defending their own self-esteem rather than negotiating for what they want.

There also is a third effect. Sometimes the critic is using the criticism to put the other person on the defensive to avoid real negotiation about the issue at hand. If the critic finds that this strategy does not work, he will be less likely to continue it over the long run. Thus the critic is helped to attain more facilitative messages himself.

A final effect of Agreeing with Part of a Criticism or Argument is that when the other person hears his gripe or his point acknowledged and agreed with, he knows that he has been heard and thus is relieved of the need to continually repeat his complaint or argument or to feel frustrated by the other's not listening. Just as when Reflections are used, he has the satisfaction of knowing that his message was received.

Agreeing with Part of a Criticism or Argument in and of itself can be an extremely great addition to communication even when only one of the two partners starts to use it. It shifts the focus of the talk from who's good and bad (that is, who gets the spanking and who gets the ice-cream cone from the imaginary parent) to a negotiation of wants.

7. Asking for More Specific Criticism

Definition: When you use this response to a criticism or challenge or argument, you ask your critic to give you more information and to make his criticism more specific.

There are three types of Asking for More Specific Criticism: (1) asking what specific behaviors the critic didn't like, (2) asking what specific behaviors the critic would have wanted or would want in the future, and (3) asking what aspects of your behaviors the critic didn't like—finding out the meaning of the behavior that gave it its negative connotation.

Examples: John has said, "You don't have any sense, Mary." Mary replies, "Is there some particular thing I've done that you didn't like?" She is Asking for More Specific Criticism.

Bill has said, "You're doing that all wrong, Mary." Mary replies, "What would you like me to be doing instead?" She is Asking for More Specific Criticism.

Aunt Martha has said, "You always used to come visit us every weekend. I don't know what's happened to you that you've become so inconsiderate." Mary replies, "What is it about my not coming so often that bothers you, Aunt Martha?" She is Asking for More Specific Criticism.

Effects: Asking for More Specific Criticism can turn a nonproductive argument into a productive negotiation session. When you ask for more specific criticism you get the other person to communicate exactly what behaviors she wants changed, what behaviors she wants in their place, and what it is about the unwanted behaviors that is unpleasant. With this information, something can be done to remedy the situation. When you hear this specific information, you are able to bargain with the other person—"I hear you wanting me to do this. Will you do this for me in return if I do that?" Or if you have no intention of doing what the other person wants, you can be open with the other person about what you will do.

By not disputing the criticism, at least not until it is fully heard, you preclude an escalation of anger. You avoid getting into an argument with the critic. You help your critic define his task not as proving you wrong or bad, but of giving you helpful information as clearly as possible.

The critic also gets a clear message of your willingness to listen and your interest. Again, here is a force turning hostility into negotiation.

8. *Listing Options and Choosing among Them*

Definition: This is a more complicated technique than the ones I have given up to now because it involves both people. It is especially useful when your wants conflict with another person's wants. The two of you get together and go through these six steps:

1. Define the problem. Each person gives his viewpoint, and allows the other to make Reflections. Continue

until it is very clear what problem is on the agenda.

2. Generate as many alternative solutions as you can think of, preferably *without* evaluating them at the time.
3. Go back and evaluate these options.
4. Select one of them, or a set of them, to try.
5. Try it.
6. Get back together and talk about how well it worked, and do the whole process over again if improvement is needed.

Example: The following interaction between Mary and Bill illustrates Listing Options and Choosing among Them.

Step one:

Mary: "Bill, I think we have a conflict of interests tonight. You always watch the basketball game from 8:30 to 9:30, and tonight I want to watch *Hamlet* on TV on a different station at that time."

Bill: "Yes, we do have a conflict of interests because I'm really interested in seeing the game tonight. Shall we figure out our options, and see which one we both want to try?"

Step two:

Mary: "OK, one option is that you could not watch the game."

Bill: "That's right. Another option is that you could not watch your show. Or, you could buy us another TV set."

Mary: "Or one of us could go over to Ralph and Betty's place and see if you could watch the game on their set."

Bill: "Or if they aren't in, one of us could go over to Aunt Ella's house; she hardly ever uses her TV."

Mary: "Or if worse comes to worse you could go down to the local bar, where they always have the game on the TV."

Bill: "Or we could go out skiing together, which we haven't done in a while, and neither one of us watch TV."

Mary: "That seems like enough alternatives to me. Does it to you?"

Bill: "Yes."

Step three:

Mary: "Well, let's see. I'd like to go skiing soon, but not tonight, because I really want to see this version of the movie."

Bill: "We really might give some thought to getting another cheap TV, but I think tonight is too soon for that solution."

Mary: "That leaves one of us to find another place to watch the show; I'd prefer to stay home tonight if possible, but I'd also be willing to be the one that goes."

Bill: "I'd prefer to stay home, too, but I'm willing to go tonight if you'll be willing to do it the next time this comes up."

Step four:

Mary: "That sounds fair. Would you like for me to do the phone calling for you?"

Bill: "Yeah, that'd be nice. Try Ralph and Betty first, and then Aunt Ella if you can't get them."

Step five:

Mary and Bill do as they planned. Mary finds out that Betty wants to see *Hamlet* and that Ralph wants to watch the game, so they switch off and each watches the show he wants to see.

Step six (afterwards):

Bill: "How'd that work out for you?"

Mary: "Great! Betty and I had a good time, and the movie was fantastic. How about you?"

Bill: "Fine, except for a little trouble with Ralph and Betty's dog."

Mary: "Oh? Tell me about it so that I can be prepared when next time comes and I go over there."

Effects: The method tends to get two people into a

cooperative frame of mind rather than a competitive one. They use their talents trying to think of creative solutions rather than trying to impose upon the other person the first option that comes to mind. Since both people create the list of options, they avoid the sense that one is winning and the other is losing when the final course of action is chosen. And since they have built into the system the idea of reevaluating the solution after it is tried, neither feels stuck or committed to something that can't be reversed. They define the problem as figuring out a solution acceptable to both; both have won when this happens and neither has won until it happens. Thus the two work as a team to solve the problem: they are not on separate teams battling each other.

When solving problems by Listing Options and Choosing among Them, each person will do best to restrain herself from evaluating an option until the two have both finished listing all that they can think of for the time being. *Then* is the best time to go back and evaluate which ones they like or don't like.

Why keep the listing and evaluating separate? There are several reasons. First, the absence of evaluation, even for a little while, helps you feel free to pose options—you know that an option won't be rejected or ridiculed, at least not until there are others to balance it off. Second, more options get brought up this way. Otherwise people tend to get into evaluation and forget to go back to thinking of more options; they tend to stop listing options too soon because they're sidetracked onto evaluation. Third, when a list is made up by the two people, with neither of them commenting pro or con on any option, both tend to lose some of their personal investment in any one option. By evaluation time, each may have already started to forget who suggested which option. At any rate, the necessity to save face by getting one's option accepted is reduced, since there is a list of options. Both people realize that most will be rejected and that it is not a disgrace to have any one option rejected.

The habit of responding positively or negatively to each option as it is brought up is very strong for most people. It is helpful, though not absolutely necessary, to overcome this habit.

9. Bargaining

Definition: When making a Bargaining response, a communicator offers to sacrifice for the other if the other will sacrifice for him in return.

Examples: "OK, I'm hearing that it doesn't help for me to nag you about your drinking. If I work on quitting doing that, will you work on telling me something nice more often?"

"One possibility is that I go with you to the ball game tonight, and you go over with me and have supper with my parents next Sunday. How does that sound?"

"If I stop bothering you about staying out late and waking me up when you come in, will you agree to cook a meal for me the next day, every time it happens?"

"Let's make a deal: if you'll work on being more honest about your feelings with me, I'll work on not reacting so extremely when you say something negative."

"I'd like for you to stop playing your stereo loudly after ten-thirty at night. I know this is a sacrifice for you; can you think of anything I can do for you in return, to make it worthwhile?"

Effects: The technique of Bargaining allows both people to sacrifice some and get more in return. Each gives up something of less value and gets something of more value.

Very frequently, couples get into a situation where one sacrifices for the other and feels resentful while the other feels guilty about receiving a sacrifice. As a result of this situation, both become hesitant to ask anything of the other, and neither gets what he wants from the other. The technique of Bargaining allows the couple to escape this stifling arrangement, negotiate more freely, and meet each other's wants creatively.

Bargaining is the classic example of offering positive, rather than negative incentives. If you do what I want, I'll give you a carrot; I won't hit you with a stick if you don't.

10. Quantification of Wants and Feelings

Definition: In order to communicate more precisely how much you want or feel something, you rate the want or feeling on a numerical scale of 0 to 10, or a verbal scale of "slightly," to "moderately," to "greatly," to "extremely."

Examples: "I'd really rather not get such a big car. And I have a pretty strong preference—about 8 out of 10."

"I'd prefer to play tennis, by about 2 on a scale of 10."

"I want you to quit being sarcastic like that, and I want it about 10 on a scale of 10!"

"I mind only a little that you were late—about 1 on a scale of 10."

"I mind only very slightly that you were late."

Effects: Ordinary language customs have not evolved reliable and precise ways of expressing *degrees* of feelings. Often people say, "I'm not angry," because if they say, "I'm angry," the hearer will think they are *very* angry. Or they will say, "I don't care. What do you want to do?" because if they say, "I'd prefer to play tennis," the other will think they are insisting rather than stating a mild preference.

On the other hand, if someone *strongly* wants something, he often thinks he has to bang on the table or start screaming to express the degree of his wanting, or in more extreme cases, to threaten to cut off the relationship or make a suicidal or homicidal gesture.

The quantification technique allows you to communicate not only the preference or feeling, but also how *strong* it is, in a precise way, without needing to play the games I've just mentioned. This is especially true when the other person learns to hear and heed the quantifications.

11. Self-disclosure

Definition: A Self-disclosure is a statement in which you openly and nonapologetically reveal something somewhat private about yourself. This can be a want or a feeling—the I Want and I Feel statements are special cases of Self-disclosure—or it can be a past action, an intention, a fantasy, an event, an ability, etc.

Examples: "One summer I worked for an insulation company, and I hated every minute of it."

"When you were speaking just then I'll have to confess my mind was a thousand miles away."

"I don't know anything at all about that subject."

"When I was a child, I used to steal my brother's lunch all of the time."

"I don't intend to ever get married again, unless things change a lot. I think I'm scared to."

"Something happened today that made me really upset . . . ."

"Yes, I'm a pretty good piano player."

"You remember what I told you about that a while back? It wasn't true."

Effects: We often avoid getting to know each other by talking only about things totally external to ourselves. We are sometimes afraid that if we reveal "private" information about ourselves, the other person may be shocked or turned off or have some other negative reaction.

It is true that the other person may have a negative

reaction. But one of the most important dimensions of growth is the ability to tolerate and accept, for the time being, all the various aspects of ourselves, those that need to be changed as well as those that need to be kept as they are. And if you make self-disclosures in an open, confident, nonapologetic tone of voice, not avoiding eye contact, it is surprising how often the feared negative reactions do not come.

When two people are able to freely self-disclose, they are closer to intimacy and full experiencing of each other.

12. Speaking about External Events

Definition: This type of statement is the opposite of Self-disclosure. It is a statement about something in the external world, something that is not private or personal.

Examples: "So then I went to the next doctor, who said he could see me on Tuesday. But I couldn't come on Tuesday, so we decided he'd see me on the next Friday. . . ."

"It's a movie about a man who is taking a trip to see his son graduate; while he's taking the trip he has all sorts of memories and dreams . . . ."

"My job has been going pretty well lately—we haven't had much work this last week, but we're expecting the real crunch to come as Christmas starts getting closer. . . ."

"It's got 80,000 miles on it, but it's still running perfectly—a little work on the carburetor a few months ago, but . . . ."

Effects: When you are just getting to know someone, Speaking about External Events is a "safe" way of getting familiar. Some people may be made uncomfortable by a high degree of self-disclosure too soon. And in ordinary "social" conversation it is a staple.

For people who already know each other, however,

Speaking about External Events is often used as a defense against getting to a discussion of the real issues in their lives. Thus I include it in the facilitative message list, and also include Excessive Speaking about External Events in the obstructive message list.

Exercise 3
Labeling Facilitative Messages

Each of the following statements is an example of one of these types:

> Agreeing with Part of a Criticism or Argument
> Asking for More Specific Criticism
> Listing Options and Choosing among Them
> Bargaining
> Quantification of Wants and Feelings
> Self-disclosure
> Speaking about External Events
> Reflection

Identify each numbered I Feel statement as an example of one of the above. Answers, if you need them, are at the end of the exercise.

1. Mary says, "That sure was good food, wasn't it? I don't think I've ever had spinach souffle like that. What a fine restaurant."

2. Bill replies, "Mr. Rupert thinks it's the best in town, and I wouldn't argue with him on that. They sure do charge enough, though! Four dollars for four snails!"

3. Mary says, "Bill, something bothered me when we were out eating with Fred and Margaret then; the way you tell stories irritates me somewhat. It's not a whole lot, maybe about 4 on a scale of 10."

4. Bill says, "I guess the way I tell stories can be irritating sometimes."

5. Bill continues, "What was it in particular that irritated you?"

6. Mary replies, "When you tell the same stories that I've already heard so many times, and when you take a long time in telling them, I begin to feel bored; not extremely so, but just enough to feel unpleasant."

7. Bill replies, "So what you don't like is how I keep telling the same ones, and that I take too long in telling them?" (Mary nods.)

8. Bill says, "Well, you're right. I do do both of those things, and I can see how it might be boring for you."

9. Bill continues, "The way that you react during my stories sometimes bothers me a lot, sometimes as much as say 8 on a scale of 10."

10. Mary replies, "You mean the way I act when we're out with people and you're telling a story gets to you?" Bill nods yes.

11. Mary continues, "What is it about my reaction that bothers you?"

12. Bill says, "When you drum your fingers on the table and sigh and stare off into space, and especially when you look at someone else and shake your head, that hurts my feelings."

13. Mary replies, "So you're saying that you could already tell that I wasn't enjoying your stories, and the way I looked bored hurt you?"

14. Bill nods yes and says, "I knew that something was wrong, but I never was too sure exactly what. I thought maybe my tone of voice. I don't know why I never asked."

15. Mary says, "I guess I wasn't quite aware of doing those things so obviously, but thinking back, I can remember doing them. You're right. I guess that wasn't the best way of letting you know."

16. Bill says, "Let's figure out some options that we have for a new arrangement so that we don't stay in the same pattern that we're in now."

17. Mary says, "OK, one option is that you could work on

telling fewer of the same stories, and tell them quicker, in return for my not looking so obviously bored."

18. Bill says, "Another option is that when I am not boring you, you could smile and wink at me or something, or tell me later, so that I'll know that I'm on target with what you like."

19. Mary says, "Or another option is that I could give you a kick under the table when I'm getting bored, instead of doing those things that I do now. Or, now that I know that the way I react bothers you 8 on a scale of 10, and now that I've told you how I feel, I'd be willing to just put up with your stories in return for your putting up with some of the irritating things that I haven't stopped doing."

20. Bill says, "It feels good to hear that you would be willing to do that because I'm in the habit awfully strongly, and it's kind of scary to think of having to change overnight."

21. Mary says, "Is that the option that you'd like, then?"

Bill replies, "No, I'd like to try telling fewer of the same stories and telling them quicker when I do, in return for your letting me know when you liked it and weren't bored. How is that with you?"

Mary replies, "That sounds good. Let's try it the next time we get together with friends, and talk over how it went afterwards."

Bill says, "OK," and then they go back to talking about souffles; Mary explains to Bill what the difference is between souffle and a truffle, and Bill practices at telling very quickly the joke about the truffle that liked to scuffle.

Answers to Exercise 3

1. Speaking about External Events
2. Speaking about External Events
3. I Feel statement, Quantification of Feelings

4. Agreeing with Part of Criticism
5. Asking for More Specific Criticism
6. I Feel statement
7. Reflection
8. Agreeing with Part of Criticism
9. I Feel statement, Quantification of Feelings
10. Reflection
11. Asking for More Specific Criticism
12. I Feel statement
13. Reflection
14. Self-disclosure
15. Agreeing with Part of Criticism, Self-disclosure
16. Introducing Listing Options and Choosing among Them
17. Bargaining, Listing Options
18. Listing Options
19. Listing Options, Bargaining
20. I Feel statement, Self-disclosure
21. Conclusion of Listing Options and Choosing among Them

Exercise 4
Making up Facilitative Messages

Make up three or four examples of each of the following facilitative formats and imagine yourself saying them to someone. Which are currently in your repertoire, and which seem new to you?

Agreeing with Part of a Criticism or Argument
Asking for More Specific Criticism
Listing Options and Choosing among Them
Bargaining
Quantification of Wants and Feelings
Self-disclosure
Speaking about External Events

We now continue with facilitative messages.

13. Citing Specific Behaviors and Observations

Definition: This technique consists of naming specific behaviors and events and describing them in sensory images so the other person knows exactly what behaviors or observations you are talking about.

Examples: "I liked it the other day when you asked me not to interrupt you; I thought that was honest and straightforward." (As opposed to, "I like it when you're honest with me.")

"George, I noticed that you weren't saying much, you weren't smiling, and when anyone asked you a question you would say, 'Oh, I don't know' or something. I'm wondering what was going on?" (As opposed to, "I noticed that you were angry, and I'm wondering why?")

"I wish that you would call me up and let me know when you're going to be late in getting home." (As opposed to, "I wish that you were more considerate.")

"Of the three times I've seen Jim, twice he had a bottle with him and acted drunk." (As opposed to, "Jim is a drunk.")

Effects: We communicate concerning observations and inferences. An observation is what we see, hear, feel, taste or smell in the outside world or find in ourselves by introspection. An inference is a more abstract thought adding some meaning to the observations. People may disagree, or miscommunicate, on the observations themselves, or even if they agree on the observation, they may disagree or miscommunicate on the inferences from the observations. With each added layer of higher abstraction, as the speakers get further away from pure reporting of observations, there is increased opportunity for disagreement and miscommunication.

For example, in the second example above, George, the person addressed, might agree with the observations that he wasn't smiling, that he wasn't saying much, and that he responded with short answers to questions. These are sensory data available to both persons. However, he might not agree to the statement that he was angry—this is an inference. He might state that he was tired, sick, or totally involved in working on an intellectual problem and not the least bit angry. He can report observations on his internal mental state, whereas the other person can only make inferences.

If people first communicate their observations, they can then go on to the inferences knowing they are starting from the same place. What often happens is that people speak in terms of inferences without ever stating the observations they were based on. Then if they disagree or misunderstand, it is very difficult for them to figure out where in the process of observing and inferring that their disagreement took place.

Another rationale for Citing Specific Behaviors is as follows. One of the purposes of communication is to make requests that the receiver either change behavior or continue a certain behavior. And when you cite specific behaviors to me, I know exactly what you want changed or continued. On the other hand, when you use words like "considerate" and "kind" and the like, I get only a vague and general idea of what you want. My idea of considerateness may be very different from yours.

14. Expressing Mixed Feelings

Definition: When Expressing Mixed Feelings, you respond to a certain event, naming more than one feeling and explaining where each is coming from.

Examples: (Pat's mother is concerned that Pat hasn't been getting enough sleep and keeps worrying herself and Pat about this.) Pat says, "Mother, I feel grateful that you're concerned about me; it's nice to know that you care. It also makes me feel insulted a little that you don't feel like I can take care of myself, and I get annoyed when you keep bringing the subject up." Either one of these feelings without the other would be an incomplete picture and would leave Pat feeling uncomfortable with the communication.

(Ralph's fellow worker points out a mistake that Ralph has been making in the bookkeeping and suggests some changes that will be very helpful. However, she does this in a very superior and condescending tone of voice, with frequent You Are Bad and You Should sentences.) Ralph says, "The way you've told me this—your tone of voice and your use of You Should's—makes me feel put down and condescended to. But you've given me some very helpful information and I'm grateful for that."

Effects: Sometimes when we have mixed feelings, no communication takes place at all. Ralph, for example, might have felt that he had no right to express his put-down feelings because he "should" be grateful, and might have been unwilling to express his grateful feelings because he felt put down. If he is comfortable with expressing both positive and negative feelings in response to the same incident, his ability to communicate is vastly increased. His fellow worker then knows that her action was neither all pleasant nor all unpleasant to Ralph. She knows that he wants her to keep making intelligent suggestions but to do it in a different way. Without the ability to express mixed feelings, Ralph would have had no option but to totally accept or totally reject her behavior.

15. Asking for Feedback

Definition: Asking for Feedback is asking for the other person's reaction to what you have just said.

Examples: ("My desire is that we not spend any money on clothes or restaurants for at least a couple of months,"

Jim has just said.) Then he says, "What's your reaction to that?"

"What do you think about what I just said?"
"I'm interested in how you react to that idea."
"How does that make you feel to hear me saying that?"
"What are your ideas about that?"

Effects: This technique is the opposite of "hit and run" tactics or overlong statements. It encourages the other person to "check out" by a Reflection, to express feelings, and otherwise to give you feedback. This feedback serves at least two functions. First, it may be beneficial information in its own right. Second, it allows you to make sure that the message is being received as you meant it to be received; if it isn't, you can try again right then rather than live with the miscommunication until it happens to get cleared up. This message is especially useful when people complain there is no dialogue, but only a series of monologues. It is useful as an antidote to patterns of avoidance of communication on important issues.

16. Nonverbal "I'm OK, You're OK" Messages

Definition: When you send Nonverbal "I'm OK, You're OK" messages, you use your vocal inflection, body posturing, volume of speech, and eye contact to say that "I am accepting of myself, even though I know I have faults and make mistakes, and I am accepting of you, even though you also are imperfect." Your voice is comfortably loud and does not trail off at the end of the sentence. You maintain eye contact a substantial part of the time, though you don't stare. Your posture is relaxed, upright and not overly protective of the chest, abdomen, and genital regions.

Examples: (Pat comes home and smells smoke. Pat says, "Hmm, I smell smoke.")

Lee replies, "I was cooking some rolls and forgot them, and they burnt to a crisp." (Lee says this looking Pat in the eye, smiling slightly, facing Pat head on, standing up straight, speaking in a moderately loud voice. The pitch at the end of the sentence signals a clear and definite stop.)

Contrast this with the different communication: "Uh, well, I was cooking some rolls, and I guess I forgot them, and they burned . . . " in which Lee gets quieter and quieter, faces sideways more and more, avoids Pat's eyes, and ends the sentence with a pitch implying there is more to come but Lee can't think of an excuse.

Contrast both of these with a different communication: Lee yells at Pat, "I was cooking some rolls and forgot them, and they burned!" spoken in a challenging tone, with both arms flared back as if to be ready to take a swing, with a frowning facial expression, and a rapid forward lean as the utterance is made. The first of the three communicates, "I'm OK, You're OK," the second communicates "I'm not OK," the third communicates "You're not OK."

Effects: Using the terms popularized by the trans-actional analysts, communication takes place best under assumptions of "I'm OK, You're OK," by each person. Non-verbal messages often communicate these stances, and trying on the nonverbal accoutrements of the self-accepting, other-accepting stance can help you operate from that stance.

When I send you a non-self-accepting, "I'm not OK" message, you may often feel the need to chastise or reassure me—my self-effacing posture tells you I am a child in need of a parent. When, on the other hand, you get a nonaccepting "You're not OK" message from me, you may often feel the need to defend yourself. With self-accepting, other-accepting messages, these unnecessary tasks can be avoided, and people can get on with what they really want to do (for instance, cook some more rolls and eat that good supper that Lee's been working on).

Advocating this stance is not to say that you should try to keep your body fixed in any one posture all the time. When I'm scared or angry, I don't try to keep from looking that way! I'm not trying to turn you into an "I'm OK, You're OK" robot!

17. You Are Good, You Did Something Good, Your Something Is Good Statements

Definition: These messages are statements of the form, you are *this*, or you did *that*, or this thing of yours is *this*, where *this* and *that* by their connotations are "good" or "worthwhile."

Examples: "You handled that situation in a way that you would have been afraid to handle it before—you've really grown."

"You're getting better and better at singing those high notes—that's real progress."

"The report that you did was just exactly what we want—very proficient in every way."

"You have a real talent for thinking of unusual and stimulating fantasies, you know?"

"That was good!"

Effects: These statements, along with I Like statements and positive I Feel statements, recognize and draw attention to positive aspects of the other person and thus usually make the other feel good. They provide a reinforcer, or a reward, that might make that behavior more enjoyable for the other in the future.

You Are Good statements tend to have more of an authoritative, parental, judgmental connotation than do I Feel statements. For example, "When you sing, I really enjoy it a lot," lets me know I produced good feelings in one person, whereas, "You have a very good voice" gives me more of a judgment about myself, as compared to other singers. The first expresses the feelings of one person; the second implies more of an authoritative evaluation. I would tend to hope for the first from a friend and the second from a judge at an audition.

However, with positive statements this difference tends to be rather unimportant, and upon hearing either one of them, I'd feel good and would not worry about it! On the other hand, this difference becomes important when it comes to negative statements; a You Are Bad statement produces different effects than an I Feel statement, as we will discuss later.

18. Mutual Topic Finding

Definition: A statement or question which expresses a wish to discuss a certain topic and checks out the willingness of the other to do likewise is Mutual Topic Finding.

Examples: "Before we get into that, can we finish discussing the problem of the typewriter noise?"

"Would you like to talk about finances some now?"

"I'd like to talk with you some about how our relationship is going, OK?"

"Do you feel like talking about what the doctor told you?"

"I'd like for us not to talk about food at this meal so we cannot interrupt this fun political debate we're having. Is that OK with you?"

Effects: Sometimes people automatically and intuitively seem to want to discuss the same topic. If so, this type of message is unnecessary. However, on many occasions topics are dwelt on too long, too short, not at all, or not at the right time for the preferences of the other. To avoid this frustration, it makes sense to negotiate openly (and hopefully quickly) about the topic of discussion, just as any other issue is negotiated.

19. I Intend Statements

Definition: A statement of the form, "I intend to do this," or "I am going to do this," is an I Intend statement.

Examples: "I don't intend to punish myself over making that mistake that upset you, but I do intend to be more careful in the future."

"I intend to sell my clarinet."

"I am really exhausted and intend to sleep the whole afternoon."

Effects: In every relationship, it is necessary for each partner to be able to make some decisions independently, to run certain areas of his life without asking the other for help or consent or advice. When each person is capable of getting many of her wants met independently, then the two people are more likely to be happy with each other. They thus avoid a situation in which each is expecting the other to make life happy for her.

I Intend statements will probably elicit hostility from the other when they are used in decisions which the other would like to be made jointly. For example, the statement, "I intend that the two of us go over to see my mother," would probably evoke some anger, whereas the statement, "I would like for the two of us to see my mother," would probably not. Thus in choosing when to use I Intend statements versus I Want statements, the person is choosing whether she thinks a decision is best made independently or in negotiation with the other.

20. Communication Postponement

Definition: A Communication Postponement is a special type of I Want statement, one that asks for a postponement of the discussion until a certain time when circumstances are more favorable. For example, if one person feels so angry or hurt that he feels like walking out of the room and slamming the door, or hitting the other person, or hanging up the telephone, it may be a good idea for both to take some time to regain composure.

Examples: "I'm feeling very hurt and angry right now and would like some time to relax before we try to work out a solution to this. Can I talk to you tomorrow night at the same time?"

"We've been working on this a long time, and I'm feeling very fatigued. I'd like to go out and walk around by myself for an hour or two and then maybe work on solving this some more."

Effects: Sometimes communicating on highly emotionally charged issues can get so unpleasant or tiring that one or both people need to rest and recuperate before adaptive communication can be kept up. Often a hostile gesture is made at such a time, such as hanging up the telephone or walking out of the room—these are called Communication Cutoffs. If the person can realize that it is OK to be tired or to need to be alone, he can avoid a Communication Cutoff by openly negotiating for a postponement.

Exercise 5
Labeling Facilitative Messages

Each of the following statements is an example of one of these types:

Citing Specific Behaviors and Observations
Expressing Mixed Feelings

Asking for Feedback
Nonverbal "I'm OK, You're OK" Messages
You Are Good, You Did Something Good, or Your Something Is Good
Mutual Topic-Finding
I Intend statement
Communication Postponement

Label these messages. Answers, if you need them, are at the end of the exercise.

Situation: Jed and Mike are in a department where two of their employees, John and Mary, have been having trouble getting along.

1. Jed says, "Mike, do you have a few minutes to talk about the problem with John and Mary?" Mike nods yes.

2. Jed continues, "I've been thinking that maybe one of us had better tell John and Mary that if they can't stop bickering with each other, they are both in danger of losing their jobs. What's your reaction to that?"

3. Mike replies, "Jed, I feel uneasy about making them fear losing their jobs, but I am glad you are concerned about the problem, and I'm glad you brought it up so we can think about it some more."

4. Jed replies, "I've felt uneasy about the idea of threatening them with losing their jobs too, Mike, and I sure am interested in other solutions if we can think of some." Jed says this with a lively and interested facial expression, maintaining eye contact with Mike while saying it, and in a tone of voice that is enthusiastic, not self-effacing or accusing.

5. Mike says, "Jed, you're always open-minded, and you do a better job because of it."

6. Jed grins. Mike continues, "One option I've thought of is that we could bow out of the job of trying to intervene in their disputes and not worry about getting them

settled. We could just let them settle all their own disputes and let it be their problem, and not ours." Mike says this in a positive, enthusiastic tone, making eye contact with Jed.

7. Jed replies, "In other words, if one comes complaining about the other, to say, 'See what the two of you can work out'?"

8. Mike says, "Yes," and then says, "What's your reaction to that?"

9. Jed says, "Humh, I like the idea of our getting less involved, because I think our habit of taking sides might even encourage them to get into fights and then come to us. But I still feel uneasy, and unsatisfied, because they also cause problems with the other employees, and our staying out of it might not solve that problem."

10. Mike says, "Another option that I intend to try is to give both of them more reward and recognition, since both of them seem to need a lot more than they're getting and a lot of their fights seem to have something to do with that."

11. Mike continues, "By reward and recognition, I mean, for example, telling them they did a good job on something, or writing them a memo saying they did well, or actually giving them a pat on the back, and doing these especially when they've worked well together."

12. Jed says, "When you say that you think their fights have to do with their needing more recognition than they're getting, are you talking about times like last Monday, when John wanted Mary to do more work on that progress report, because he felt he'd done more than his fair share of the work on the project? That would be an example of his wanting recognition for what he'd done?"

13. Mike replies, "You've picked up *exactly* on what I'm talking about."

14. Jed says "Mike, I think both of your ideas are good ones and are worth trying."

15. Mike says, "Do you want to decide at this point how we're going to bow out of the role of mediator with them? Do you want to talk about whether to have a meeting with them, or for us just to change without telling them?"
16. Jed says, "Mike, you've shed some new light on this issue for me."
17. Jed continues, "I want to let these new ways of looking at it percolate in my mind some more, and then maybe at lunch tomorrow we can talk about it some more. Is that OK with you?"

As the story ends, Mike says Yes to Jed's proposal. Both of them study this book some more during their evening hours, and they list more options tomorrow.

Answers to Exercise 5

1. Mutual Topic-Finding
2. Asking for Feedback
3. Expressing Mixed Feelings
4. Nonverbal "I'm OK, You're OK" Messages
5. You Are Good, You Did Something Good
6. Nonverbal "I'm OK, You're OK" Messages (and Listing Options)
7. Citing Specific Behaviors (and a Reflection)
8. Asking for Feedback
9. Expressing Mixed Feelings
10. I Intend statement
11. Citing Specific Behaviors and Observations
12. Citing Specific Behaviors and Observations (and a Reflection)
13. You Did Something Good statement
14. Your Something Is Good statement
15. Mutual Topic-Finding
16. You Did Something Good

17. Communication Postponement (Asking for Feedback also present in this statement.)

Exercise 6
Making up Facilitative Messages

Make up three or four examples of each of the following facilitative messages and imagine yourself saying them to someone.

Citing Specific Behaviors and Observations
Expressing Mixed Feelings
Asking for Feedback
Nonverbal "I'm OK, You're OK" Messages
You Are Good, You Did Something Good, Your Something Is Good statements
Mutual Topic-Finding
Communication Postponement

4 Obstructive Messages

Now we begin to examine obstructive messages. See if you agree with me that in most interactions, substituting a facilitative message for any of these obstructive ones makes things better for all concerned.

1. Communication Cutoffs

Definition: A statement or action that cuts off communication in order to avoid unpleasant feelings, without having made any plans for continuation of communication, is a Communication Cutoff. When this action is made without having consulted the other, it also is a way of expressing hostility.

Examples: "If that's the way you think about me, then just forget it! I don't ever want to see you again!" (The speaker walks out, slamming the door.)

"I don't want to talk about this anymore—good-bye." (The speaker hangs up the telephone.)

"You don't care about me, just like all of the rest of them! I could die for all you care!" (The person gets in the car and drives off.)

"Just forget it—I won't ever bring it up ever again, OK?"

"Let's just don't talk about it—I want this to be a happy time for us."

Effects: It is obviously impossible for people to negotiate with each other to get their mutual needs met if they won't keep talking and trying to communicate with each other. After a typical Communication Cutoff both partners feel hurt, angry, and frustrated. Many partners then spend much of their energy in a game of "Who's going to recontact the other first?" Avoidance of the issue and passive attack are the results of Communication Cutoffs.

International negotiations provide many examples of Communication Cutoffs. Delegations continually seem to walk out of negotiation sessions because of the shape of the table or other perceived insults or affronts. The effects here of Communication Cutoffs can be wasted lives and continued wars.

On the other hand, a Communication Postponement is, as discussed in the previous chapter, a negotiation for a postponement of the discussion until negative feelings interfere less with the communication process. The Communication Postponement, unlike a Communication Cutoff, allows for a recovery of composure and energy without antagonizing the other person by making a hostile gesture.

2. Overlong Statements

Definition: No hard and fast rules are possible, but if you take more than a minute to make a statement or series of statements without giving the other person a chance to respond, there is a fair chance that you are making an Overlong Statement.

Effects: When statements are overlong, the receiver does not have a chance to give feedback to each separate point: frequent Reflections are impossible.

When I make an Overlong Statement, your natural tendency may be to hear and remember only a portion of my message; then I end up having to repeat the other parts. Or you may have some responses you want to make at various times, and it may be frustrating for you to hold them, waiting for me to finish. You may get the notion that you, too, had better make an Overlong Statement when you get the floor because it is the only way your ideas will ever be heard. When we are giving long speeches to each other, we never know how much is being received correctly by the other.

3. Put-Down Questions

Definition: A rhetorical question, asked not to gain information but to communicate a want or a dissatisfied feeling in an indirect way, is a Put-Down Question.

Examples: "Why don't you ever dress neatly?" (The asker doesn't really care why; he is indirectly communicating that he *wants* you to dress more neatly.)

"Why can't you learn to be responsible with money?" (The asker doesn't care why you are irresponsible; she is trying to communicate a *desire* that you be responsible, or an irritated or angry *feeling* about your behavior.)

"Why should I keep on in this relationship with you when you don't put a thing into it?"

"Don't you realize that I know that?"

"Don't you think you've said enough for one night?"

"What's the use in my doing anything for you when you always screw it up anyway?"

"What kind of a fool do you think I am, anyway?"

"Must I always play mother to you?"

Effects: These questions throw off the communication process from its purpose of allowing negotiation and mutual need-meeting. They do this by inviting the other person to counterattack or defend against the veiled accusation. Or they invite the other to answer the question, which if done directly would appear ridiculous. (Example: "How many times do you expect me to put up with this?" "Oh, some-where between five and ten more times.") Since the asker does not really want an answer to the question, he would be more direct in using an I Want statement or an I Feel statement that directly expresses what's on his mind.

4. Speaking about General Ways of Being

Definition: When your message describes behavior with general words instead of specific words that can create a discrete sensory image of the behavior you are referring to, you are Speaking about General Ways of Being.

Examples: "I wish you weren't so cold." (As opposed to, "I wish you would smile and talk with me more.")

"You don't know how to handle money." (As opposed to, "You overspent your checking account three times.")

"I wish that you would not be so sensitive." (As opposed to, "I wish that you would not have such a hurt look and tone of voice when I criticize you.")

"I wish you weren't such a slob." (As opposed to, "I wish you wouldn't leave your pants on the living room floor.")

"Don't be ridiculous."

"You're being unfair."

"Why do you have to be such a jerk?"

"The thing I like about you is that you're such a good person."

Effects: One purpose of communication is to help two people let each other know what behaviors they want and don't want from each other. The general adjectives and nouns and other words used in the examples above do not clearly let the receiver know what behaviors are being referred to; thus the waters are muddied and people confuse each other. My image of "sensitive" behavior might be totally different from yours; possible "sensitive" behaviors include anything from enthusiastically talking about poetry to listening attentively to crying when criticized. Thus the effect of Speaking about General Ways of Being is a rather unenlightening exchange of emotion: the receiver never does learn exactly what she did to elicit that emotion.

The antidote to Speaking about General Ways of Being is Citing Specific Behaviors and Observations.

5a. *You Are Bad, You Did Something Bad,*
Your Something Is Bad Statements

Definition: Statements like, "You are X" or "You did X" or "This of yours is X," in which X has a negative or pejorative connotation and a negative value judgment attached to it, are You Are Bad, You Did Something Bad, or Your Something Is Bad statements. The pejorative connotations of language are used to express a want or feeling instead of talking directly about wants and feelings.

These messages include similar statements that use the past, present, or future tenses: "You will be bad" is a type of You Are Bad statement.

Examples: "You don't care about anybody but yourself!" (As opposed to, "I don't like it when you take trips without me.")

"You are just a cold person." (As opposed to, "When you don't speak to me when I walk into the room, I feel hurt.")

"You think you're a man, but you're not." (You are bad.)

"You acted like a fool at the party." (You did bad.)

"You're dishonest." (You are bad.)

"You're never going to amount to anything." (You will be, or are, bad.)

"You are just so in love with yourself." (You are bad.)

"Your speech stank." (Your something is bad.)

"That dress looks like a flour sack." (Your something is bad.)

Effects: When someone receives one of these types of statements, for example, "You acted like a fool at the party," he usually feels somewhat threatened. He is hearing an accusation that implies that his behavior is "wrong" or "foolish" in the eyes of some ultimate judge. One way to defend himself against such a threat is to try to prove that "No, I'm not bad. It's your values that are messed up, and really you are bad." So he may reply, "No, I didn't act like a fool at the party. I just had a good time. Just because you're too shy to get into the spirit, you think I should be the same way." Thus he responds to the You Are Bad statement with another You Are Bad statement, and the exchange continues along these lines. The two are acting as if there were some ultimate judge who could make a pronouncement, such as, "Here is my decision! You are bad, and you are good! You get a spanking, and you get an ice-cream cone!" But there is no ultimate judge, no parent they can run to who will decide who was right and who was wrong.

On the other hand, if the initial statement had been, "You know, right or wrong, I feel embarrassed when you yell and dance around at parties like you did tonight. If you could do that less, I'd be willing to do something for you in return—how does that sound?" Here the morality or the goodness or badness of our enthusiastic party-goer is not attacked. His self-worth is not an issue. He has simply received a request to do something different, not because what he did is bad, but because it created unpleasant feelings in the one person who is asking him to change.

Therapists find that many of their clients' problems result from scary feelings and defenses against them; these feelings often were first elicited in childhood. In adulthood, then, the words or events that evoked fear in childhood still evoke fear. You Are Bad and You Did Something Bad statements tend to bring back the scary feelings that one had in childhood when he heard his parents say, "You are Bad" and then got punished or scared. Avoiding You Are Bad and You Did Something Bad statements enables us to bypass those scary feelings as much as possible. I Want and I Feel and Bargaining can express anything that You Are Bad and You Did Something Bad statements can and are conducive to negotiation rather than counterattack, and to mutual reward rather than mutual punishment.

5b. You Should Statements

Definition: Statements like "You should do this," or "You should have done this," or "You ought not to have done this," "You have no right to do this," are You Should statements.

Examples: "You shouldn't feel so bad." (As opposed to, "I worry when I see you looking so upset.")

"You should have prepared for this long ago." (As opposed to, "I feel irritated because your lack of preparation for this makes more work for me.")

"You shouldn't have acted the way you did at the party."

"You ought to be friendlier to my parents."

Effects: The word "should" invokes the voice of conscience. Although (or perhaps because) one's conscience is perhaps one's most precious possession, people often strongly resist letting someone else speak the voice of conscience to them, particularly when they are already angry. Often it's best to bypass the struggle between conscience and the rebellion against it by speaking of wants, feelings, and effects of actions, rather than shoulds and oughts.

6. Defending Oneself

Definition: A response to a moralization or implied or expressed criticism in which the person attempts to prove that what he did was "right" or "good" or "cool" or "justified" or "acceptable under the circumstances" or otherwise conforming to the standards of some real or implied authority is Defending Oneself.

Examples: "No, it wasn't my fault that we were late. I was the one who was trying to hurry us up."

"I wasn't either disrespectful to your mother—I was just telling the truth, that's all."

"I have a right to talk however I want to your mother." Defending Oneself often is accompanied by a counterattacking You Are Bad statement, as in the following examples:

"If you weren't so neurotic, you wouldn't care whether I was fifteen minutes late or not."

"The only reason I was late was that I had to pick up the things that *you* left around the house."

"I don't know why I should talk nicer to your mother. She never did anything nice for me, or anybody else for that matter, which might be why you turned out the way you did."

Effects: Defending Oneself, with or without counterattacking with a You Are Bad statement, tends to keep the discussion on a level of what is right or justified or good according to some implied authority. When the discussion is on this level, people tend to forget that their task is to find the option that will maximize happiness for both of them and that there is no need to settle who is at fault.

Exercise 7
Labeling Obstructive Messages

Each of the statements below is an example of one of the

following:
>   Communication Cutoff
>   Put-Down Question
>   Speaking about General Ways of Being
>   You Are Bad or You Did Something Bad or Your Something Is Bad statements
>   You Should statements
>   Defending Oneself

Label each message according to one or more of the above categories. Some messages may be examples of more than one category.

1. "Patty, why can't you do your own work, so that other people can do their own without having to do yours?" says June.

2. Patty replies, "What do you think you're talking about?"

3. June replies, "I'm talking about how you're so irresponsible. It's just pitiful."

4. June continues, "You ought to have finished working on that report two weeks ago."

5. June continues, "You didn't finish it on time, and then you took off on vacation without having made any plans about it, without taking care of it in any way at all, and left it for me to do."

6. Patty replies, "So, are you getting paid for doing it or aren't you?"

7. Patty continues, "You're just griping at me because you had to do something yourself. You couldn't push it off on me like you usually do."

8. June replies, "Push it off on you? The only times I *ever* gave you any of my work to do was when you were not only willing to do it but you even *asked* me to let you do it."

9. Patty replies, "Do you expect me to let you get away with saying that? Have you totally lost your memory?"

10. At this point Frank, who has overheard the conversation from the next room, enters and says, "June, I think you're being unreasonable."
11. June replies, "Who asked you?"
12. June continues, "Why are you taking her side?"
13. June continues, "You just want to see what you can get off her. You've been getting turned on by those flirty looks she keeps giving you."
14. June continues, "Why don't you say to her face what you said about her the other day at lunch when you lechers got together?"
15. Patty gets up and stamps out of the room, slamming the door, resolving to avoid both June and Frank.
16. Frank says, "You're acting totally crazy, June."
17. Frank continues, "I wasn't taking her side, and it doesn't have anything to do with what you think it does."
18. June says, "Well then why do you keep being so meddlesome?"
19. June continues, "You should just mind your own business."
20. Frank says, "The only reason I get involved is because the noise of the argument bothers me. That's the only reason."
21. June says, "Frank, I don't think you've said an honest word today, and maybe not in your whole life."
22. Frank starts to protest, and June walks away from him, slamming the door herself.

As our story ends, Frank turns to the audience and says, "Why do these things always happen to me?" and he resolves to go and get himself a drink.

Answers to Exercise 7

1. Put-Down Question, Speaking about General Ways of Being

2. Put-Down Question
3. You Are Bad, Speaking about General Ways of Being
4. You Should
5. You Did Something Bad
6. Put-Down Question
7. You Did Something Bad
8. Defending Oneself
9. Put-Down Question
10. You Are Bad, Speaking about General Ways of Being
11. Put-Down Question
12. Put-Down Question
13. You Did Something Bad
14. Put-Down Question
15. Communication Cutoff
16. You Did Something Bad, Speaking about General Ways of Being
17. Defending Oneself
18. Put-Down Question, Speaking about General Ways of Being
19. You Should
20. Defending Oneself
21. You Did Something Bad
22. Communication Cutoff

Exercise 8
Thinking up Examples of
Obstructive Messages

Make up two or three examples of each of the following obstructive messages. Recall any real-life examples of these. What were the effects?

Communication Cutoff
Put-Down Question
Speaking about General Ways of Being
You Are Bad statements
You Did Bad statements
Your Something Is Bad statements

7. Sarcasm

Definition: Sarcasm is making a witty or humorous comment, usually the opposite of what is meant, as a way of expressing hostility.

Examples: "Do you think you've yelled at me enough? I mean, I might need some more today to meet my minimum daily requirement."

"Oh, *sure,* you're *never* late. We all really believe that one!"

"Thanks a lot. You're real nice. So nice it almost makes me want to cry."

"Real good supper you've fixed for us tonight. Maybe I'll stop off at McDonald's on the way home from now on."

"No, I don't mind your whining. It's music to my ears! Please keep it up!"

"Did you know that what you're supposed to do is hit the ball? You know, with the strings? Most of the time the air from the racket swing is not enough to get it back."

Effects: Sarcasm allows the sender of the message to avoid responsibility for the hostile feelings—he can always say, "Oh, I was just joking." The receiver of the sarcastic message is most often moved to think of a sarcastic comeback or a counterattack of some sort, rather than to make any change in the behavior in question. If the receiver lacks the quick wit to make a suitable comeback, he often feels angry at his more powerful opponent, jealous of his opponent's humorous abilities, and desirous of meeting his opponent on a different battlefield. Thus sarcasm promotes attack and defense rather than negotiation.

8. Commanding

Definition: Commanding is directing another person to do something in an authoritarian tone that implies that the person has no choice.

Examples: "You're *not* going out tonight, and that's all there is to it."
"Turn off that record player right now."
"I don't allow smoking in my house."
"You can't do that sort of thing around here."
"Get that smile off your face right now."

Effects: The person who is commanded realizes, on some level, that the commander is setting himself up as a more powerful person. He often feels resentment about this and/or feels a desire to use some power to depose the commander. Power struggles are thus elicited by Commanding. If, on the other hand, the person commanded has no problem with passively following his commands, he has often acquired this ability at the expense of his own individuality and initiative.

9. Verbal-Nonverbal Incongruity

Definition: The sender communicates something by his facial expression, tone of voice, or body language but does not lay his cards on the table by backing it up with a verbal message of the same meaning. Or even more confusing, his nonverbal message contradicts his verbal message.

Examples: "That's OK, go on and go without me. I'll be perfectly happy here by myself at home. Don't worry about me." (spoken in a very bitter, self-pitying tone)
"No, I'm not upset, I'm OK. I feel perfectly fine, and everything is all right." (spoken in a self-pitying tone)

"You make up your mind. The decision is totally up to you; I'm staying out of it." (When the other person makes the "wrong" decision, the speaker, looking very disappointed and shocked, says, "What, you decided that?" and has a contemptuous facial expression.)

"If that's what you want to do, that's fine with me." (spoken in a tone of voice that says, "If you want to act like a fool, I can't stop you.")

"I'd really like to go out with you, but somebody else asked me to do something, and I just can't get out of it." (spoken with no eye contact; never smiles at the other; makes very short replies to the other's questions, and excuses herself from the conversation as quickly as possible)

"You never show me any affection any more! You hardly even touch me like you mean it." (spoken in an angry, threatening tone of voice, and a stiff, forbidding body posture)

"No, I'm not angry at you!" (spoken in a gruff tone of voice, after the speaker has just made several sarcastic comments)

"That's OK. Go ahead and smoke, I don't mind." (The speaker then withdraws as far as possible from the smoke, fans the air, and coughs loudly.)

"I want you to be independent." (spoken just after the mother has cleaned up the son's room)

Effects: Nonverbal messages are often effective in communicating feelings, but not a very efficient way of letting the receiver know the specific behavior which elicited that feeling and the reasons why it elicited that feeling. Nor is it efficient as a way for people to arrive at creative solutions to the problems causing unpleasant feelings. In order for solutions to be arrived at efficiently, nonverbal messages need to be backed up and supported by verbal messages of the same meaning so that both channels are helping the communication rather than working against each other.

Verbal and nonverbal messages that contradict each other are often very confusing to the receiver. The receiver may respond to the situation by similar contradictory messages, perpetuating a system of mutual deception. Or the receiver may unconsciously develop a "symptom" in order to escape the conflict of the contradictory messages. For example, when someone hears "You never show me any affection!" (spoken in an angry, forbidding tone) and has any attempt at affection greeted by a stiff and rejecting posture, he or she is receiving double messages for which there is no "correct" response. If forceful messages of this sort are received repeatedly enough, impotence or vaginismus or a backache which precludes sex altogether may be the easiest way out of this "double bind."

10. Threatening

Definition: When a person makes a threat as a way of expressing a strong want or feeling, and seeing that the want is met, she is Threatening.

Examples: "If you like being with her so much, maybe we ought to just break up and not see each other any more." (As opposed to, "It hurts me a *tremendous* lot when I see you enjoying her so much because I think you like her more than me.")

"If you can't start spending more time with me, maybe I ought to just move out and go back to live with mother." (As opposed to, "I am extremely dissatisfied, 10 on a scale of 10, that you spend so little time with me!")

"If you do that one more time, you're going to wish you hadn't."

"One more time like this, and I'm leaving."

Effects: Sometimes relationships break up, and communication is cut off not because the people are happier apart but because threats of breaking off the relationship were used as a way of expressing intensity of feeling, until one partner finally felt obliged to carry out the threat after the other called his bluff.

Threats can be an adaptive part of the negotiation process, when they simply express what the person is willing to accept and what he isn't willing to accept. For example, "If you ever beat me again, I'm going to leave and not come back," might be a simple statement of fact. It is when the communicator makes a threat that is stronger than he wants, intends, or needs to carry out, for lack of a better way of expressing feelings, that the threat obstructs the meeting of wants. Many threats fit this category.

11. Expressing Dissatisfaction through a Third Party

Definition: A statement that expresses dissatisfaction not directly to the offending person, but to someone else, is Expressing Dissatisfaction through a Third Party.

Examples: "Sorry we're late. Julie never has really learned to keep appointments on time."

(At a party, someone mentions male chauvinistic attitudes.) Mary says, "Oh, John's never had any of those kinds of attitudes, oh, no." (Then looks at John in a combination of smile and sneer.)

Effects: In addition to whatever hurt comes from the expression of dissatisfaction in the first place, the receiver, if present, now has to endure the additional embarrassment of having faults exposed in front of people who may not be sympathetic. If the offending person is not present, the person Expressing Dissatisfaction through a Third Party discharges some hostility that may hurt the offender without giving her a chance to negotiate about changing the offending behavior. Thus in this message we see a combination of attack and avoidance, a combination present in many of the obstructive messages.

12. Overgeneralizing

Definition: Overgeneralizing is making a statement that is so broad that it can't be verified, as a way of avoiding a more specific statement about feelings elicited in a relationship.

Examples: "Women just can't manage money. That's all there is to it." (As opposed to, "I don't like the fact that you lost money on that deal last week.")

"You don't care anything about me. You never listen to me. Nothing I ever do is right for you." (As opposed to, "I didn't like it that you didn't listen to me just then.")

"You can't expect people who didn't graduate from high school to be worth anything." (As opposed to, "It sure does upset me that our son dropped out of high school.")

Effects: Overgeneralizing permits people to spend time arguing over issues that are largely irrelevant to their relationship or to take stands that they don't really believe as an indirect way of talking about something important. It gets people in the habit of displacing hostility onto large groups of innocent people rather than the one person who caused the hurt.

13. Preemptive Topic Shifts

Definition: A response that shifts the topic of discussion, in spite of signals that the other person wants to address it further, is a Preemptive Topic Shift.

Examples: The following interactions illustrate Preemptive Topic Shifts.

1. First person: "I've been wondering several things about our financial situation lately. . . ."

   Second person: "I have too, for sure. . . . I hope the tax check comes back soon. By the way, before I forget it, I saw Aunt Frances today and she asked about you. . . ."

2. First person: "I don't understand. You're saying that you disagree with me that astrology tells anything about people, but you still think it's a good thing?"

   Second person: "Yeah; the reason I think it's a good thing is that it helps people meet each other." (The second person takes another bite of food, while the first person thinks about this.)

   Third person: "Don't you like these beans? Did you know the beans come from the garden? Don't you think these beans are better than store-bought beans are?"

Effects: The effect of this type of response is that things never get finished or solved, and conversations don't get pursued to the point where maximum enlightenment or interest is gained. The discussion tends to have a "touch and go" character when this type of message is used widely: many topics are touched on, and then left, and the conversation bounces around. Occasionally this message is used in a totally well-meaning way by someone who has something pop into his mind and fears forgetting it if he doesn't blurt it out now. Or he has been waiting for the first lull in the conversation to be able to say it and hasn't been listening to the other people enough to judge whether or not they desire a topic shift. On other occasions, this response is a pattern for avoiding getting into any topic in anything but a superficial way for fear that a deeper pursual of the topic might lead to something threatening.

14. Ignoring Important Messages of the Other

Definition: Ignoring Important Messages of the Other is making a response that fails to deal with, or deals only minimally with, an important message sent by the other.

Examples:
1. Patient: "I keep wondering and thinking, doctor, about whether I might maybe have cancer, or get it, and what it would be like if that happened, you know?"
   Doctor: "Has your cough gotten any better?"
2. Wife: "Oh, boy, what a day I've had today!"
   Husband: "Did you remember to pick up my pants?"
3. Wife: "How are you feeling about taking that trip to the beach?"
   Husband: (looks uncertain, squirms a little, hesitates) "Well, . . . I guess it's OK—your father will be down there, and uh . . . oh well, I guess it will be all right."
   Wife: "That's good. I heard that the weather is supposed to be just perfect down there." (The wife does not address the obvious fact that the husband is uneasy about something, seemingly something to do with her father.)

Effects: When this message is used, important issues don't get dealt with unless the person being ignored can very assertively press the issue; thus this type of message is used to avoid issues.

The person being ignored is often angered at the seeming insensitivity of the other. She may get the message that she is not loved or cared about or that she is being snubbed. It is very gratifying for most people to realize that their messages are being heard, and it is frustrating to send a message and have it ignored.

15. Attacking with a New Issue

Definition: Bringing up an extraneous issue that hurts or threatens one's partner during a discussion of a separate issue before any progress is made on the first issue is Attacking with a New Issue. This maneuver is usually made in an attempt to seek protection from scary feelings by shifting blame to the other person.

Examples: "Yeah, maybe I do drink too much, but you'd drive anybody to drink. It's no coincidence that your first husband drank too much too, is it? And your mother is just the same way." (The discussion is turned in the direction of the first husband and the mother; the couple has enough to deal with at the moment without discussing them.)

"Yeah, I forgot to pick up your clothes at the cleaners. But, damn it, if you only wouldn't spend all our money, we could pay to have the clothes delivered here. And don't think that I don't know who you spend it on, either." (The pair now has to deal with the forgotten clothes, the spending of money, and the presence of an outside affair all at the same time.)

Effects: Issues that have been dragged out in the heat of the moment in the above examples are obviously important and need to be dealt with. The fact that they were uncovered in the context of a dispute over another issue shows that they have been swept under the rug in the past and need to be discussed. However, by bringing them up in the context of another dispute the couple may be "biting off more than they can chew." Each partner may dart from one issue to another, using a change of topic as a way of getting the pressure off himself and onto the other person. Unless they can stop and agree to discuss each topic one at a time, they run the risk of getting nowhere on all of them. They thus experience all the pain of being attacked on important and painful issues and none of the pleasure of coming to an understanding or agreement on any of them.

16. *Disputing Versions of Past Events*

Definition: Disputing Versions of Past Events is a response which disagrees with another person's description of what happened in the past, calls it untrue, or supplies a different description.

Examples:

1. First person: "A while earlier you said you thought I was too demanding."

   Second person: "I did *not* say that!"

   First person: "You did too. I heard you say it right here!"

2. First person: ". . . And then I got in about ten-thirty that night. . . ."

   Second person: "It was not ten-thirty. It was every bit of midnight!"

   First person: "It couldn't have been midnight, because the late movie hadn't come on yet!"

   Second person: "Yes it was. The late movie didn't come on that night until twelve-thirty."

3. John: ". . . And then Francine told Mr. Schwartz that she didn't like the pie . . . ."

   Francine: "I did not say that. I just said that I like pies with a lot of apples in them."

   John: "Francine, you know that you said you *didn't* like pies *without* many apples in them!"

Effects: Nine times out of ten what happened in the past is irrelevant anyway, and this type of response accomplishes nothing but to make both people feel bad. What *is* relevant is what the person wants or feels now about the other's behavior now and in the future. Do you *now* want me to be less demanding? Do you *now* want me to get in earlier? Do you *now* want me to apologize to Mr. Schwartz or to be more tactful in the future? These are the issues in the examples above that lead to negotiation and solving of problems.

If the two people are more interested in assigning blame for the past than in solving the problem for the future, such as in a lawsuit or trial situation, Disputing Versions of Past Events may be very useful and relevant. However, outside the courtroom, where there is no judge, the activity seldom accomplishes much.

Exercise 9
Labeling Obstructive Messages

Each of the statements below is an example of one of the following:

Sarcasm
Commanding
Verbal-Nonverbal Incongruity
Threatening
Expressing Dissatisfaction through a Third Party
Overgeneralizing
Preemptive Topic Shifts
Ignoring Important Messages of the Other
Attacking with a New Issue
Disputing Versions of Past Events

Label each statement below according to one or more of the above ten categories. Answers are at the end of the exercise.

1. Martha says, "George, tell me you love me!" (Martha says this in a Marine sergeant's tone of voice and looks rather hostile.)
2. George replies, "I *love* you, I *love* you!" (George says this in a very sour tone of voice, with a scowl on his face, as if to say, "OK, OK, already!")
3. Martha replies, "George, you're *so* romantic. I don't

think you've said anything nice to anybody in your whole life, much less felt any passion." (Actually there are several times in which George has done both of the above.)

4. George replies, "Oh, yes, Martha. I have. I remember once telling you that for a fat person you sure don't sweat very much."

5. Martha replies, "You're one to worry about my being fat, with everyone in the college community knowing that you're an alcoholic. Or at least they do after that scene at the party the night before last."

6. George replies, "It wasn't the night before last, Martha. It was three nights ago. I just adore your mental acuteness, my dear."

7. Martha yells, "Shut up! Just shut up!"

8. George says, "You're so delicate—so ladylike. That's what I love about you, Martha."

9. Martha replies, "I'd be careful what I say, lover boy. Be careful, or I'll leave you, and then you know about how long your job here at this college will last."

10. At this point Honey comes and knocks on the door, and is let in by George, who greets her saying, "Oh come in, Honey, Martha was just entertaining me with her delightful conversation. I'll let you take my place, as much as it hurts me."

11. George walks out, leaving Martha and Honey. Honey says, "Martha, it sure is good seeing you today. I'm glad to see you again." (Though Honey says this in a sincere tone, she is almost trembling with nervousness.)

12. "Heavenly," says Martha, rolling her eyes.

13. Honey says, "Some of the things George said the other night. . . . Well, there might have been a few I didn't exactly appreciate."

14. Martha says, "What would you like to drink? It's hot out there, isn't it?"

15. At this moment George walks in, wearing nothing but a

very loud bathing suit, attracting attention by walking right past Martha and Honey. In a loud voice he says, "Don't pay any attention to me. Don't let me disturb your conversation. I'm just on my way out to do some sun bathing."

16. Martha yells, "You go out there in that outfit, and you're never coming back in."

17. George says to Honey, "Martha does get in unpleasant moods. You'll have to excuse her. By the way, did you sleep well the other night after you got home? It was quite late, wasn't it?"

18. Martha says, "It wasn't night. It was morning."

19. George walks out. Honey says to Martha, "Martha, you know there's this therapy group, and everybody that ever does therapy gets true happiness. I was thinking that George. . . ."

20. Martha says, "Yes, yes. By the way, did you hear that a new professor was hired in the Sociology department?"

(The story ends by George and Martha eventually deciding to get into a communication training group. They are more satisfied afterward and only go back to their old patterns occasionally, for entertainment purposes, just to make sure they can still do it.)

Answers to Exercise 9

1. Verbal-Nonverbal Incongruity, Commanding
2. Verbal-Nonverbal Incongruity
3. Sarcasm, Overgeneralizing
4. Sarcasm
5. Attacking with a New Issue
6. Disputing Versions of Past Events, Sarcasm
7. Commanding
8. Sarcasm
9. Threatening, "Lover boy" is Sarcasm
10. Sarcasm, Expressing Dissatisfaction through a Third

Party
11. Verbal-Nonverbal Incongruity
12. Sarcasm
13. Expressing Dissatisfaction through a Third Party
14. Ignoring Important Messages of the Other, Preemptive Topic Shift
15. Verbal-Nonverbal Incongruity
16. Threatening
17. Expressing Dissatisfaction through a Third Party, Ignoring Messages of the Other, Preemptive Topic Shift
18. Disputing Versions of Past Events
19. Overgeneralizing, Expressing Dissatisfaction through a Third Party
20. Ignoring Messages of the Other, Preemptive Topic Shift

Exercise 10
Thinking up Examples of Obstructive Messages

Make up two or three examples of each of the following obstructive messages. Recall any examples from the past. What were the effects?

Sarcasm
Commanding
Verbal-Nonverbal Incongruity
Threatening
Expressing Dissatisfaction through a Third Party
Overgeneralizing
Preemptive Topic Shifts
Ignoring Important Messages of the Other
Attacking with a New Issue
Disputing Versions of Past Events

We now continue with obstructive messages.

17. Unnecessary Apologizing and Self-Effacing

Definition: When a person apologizes and blames himself not because he really believes the things he is saying, but in order to get the other person off his back, he is using Unnecessary Apologizing and Self-Effacing.

Examples: "I'm sorry I criticized you. I didn't mean it. I take it back. I won't do it again." (As opposed to, "That really bothered you when I said that, huh? I'm sorry it was so upsetting. Can you think of a way I can tell you things like that without it being so upsetting?")

Mary is very angry and starts to throw things in response to a discussion about the way John acted toward her mother. (John had told her mother that he would appreciate it if she wouldn't try to influence his job decision.) John says, "I'm sorry, Mary, I know I shouldn't have said what I said. I won't ever do it again. Will you just forgive me?" (As opposed to, "Mary, I see that what I said made you angry, but I'm not sure why. I'd like to discuss that if you would.")

Effects: When John apologizes, makes promises, and accepts blame in response to Mary's being on his back, he is teaching her that she can extract apologies and promises from him in the future by getting on his back again. Thus he is rewarding the behavior of hers that he doesn't like. In addition, he is saying things that he doesn't mean; the truth probably will come out sooner or later in some indirect way, most likely when he breaks his promises or shows that he isn't really sorry for what he did. This pattern then gets repeated, and each time negotiation about the real issue is being avoided.

18. Excessive Speaking about External Events

This form of communication was mentioned in the chapter on facilitative messages. For ordinary social conversation and the process of getting to know someone, some use of Speaking about External Events is indispensable. However, it can be used as a way of avoiding Self-disclosure and Bargaining about issues that are of importance to the relationship. In negotiation it usually interferes with the communication process when used more than occasionally.

19. Assuming Rather than Checking Out

Definition: If you assume that your perception of an ambiguous or nonverbal message was correct without checking it out verbally, you are Assuming Rather than Checking Out.

Examples: Mary and John go back to Mary's place early from a date, and Mary rushes in, saying good-bye to John in a very rushed way, looking as if she is disgusted or upset. John concludes that she doesn't like him and never asks her out again. (In fact, Mary liked John a lot. She had picked up a "bug" on a recent trip and was about to have an attack of diarrhea when they parted on the doorstep. Had he checked out her nonverbal message, he would have found that his initial perception was incorrect.)

Fred has written a poem and left it in Jean's mailbox. Later Jean passes Fred and gives him a disapproving look. He concludes that she didn't like being given the poem and feels hurt. In fact, the mail clerk put the poem in the wrong box, and the stranger who found it threw it away. Jean's disapproving look came because the pants Fred was wearing reminded her of the pants her father used to wear on fishing trips; she hated the trips. Had Fred checked out her nonverbal message, he would have found this out.

Effects: Misunderstandings persist without being cleared up. People base their actions toward others on mistaken assumptions.

20. Silent Resentment

Definition: Feeling resentment toward another person, without doing anything to change the other person's behavior or reduce one's own resentment, is Silent Resentment.

Examples: John is in the habit of interrupting Phyllis. When he does this, Phyllis inwardly fumes but says nothing. After doing a lot of silent resenting one evening, Phyllis finds herself totally unattracted to John and also develops a tension headache.

John's boss has been commanding him to hurry to meet a deadline. The boss had known of the deadline but let the work sit on his desk for several days before giving it to John. John is angry but says nothing. He comes home and flies off the handle at Phyllis for something insignificant.

Effects: Silent Resentment continued over a long time may kill warm feelings, spur psychosomatic symptoms, or spur displacement of hostility onto "innocent bystanders."

This is not to say, however, that resentment should always be expressed! Sometimes it's best to reduce the resentment, not the silence. Sometimes the best strategy for dealing with anger is to alter what you say to yourself so that you no longer feel angry. Forgiving the other person, putting the size of your injury into proper perspective, dedicating yourself toward having a good time without letting the other person spoil it, or putting your cognitive energies into finding the most rational way to behave are all strategies that can reduce resentment without ever expressing it.

21. Acting Out Anger

Definition: Doing something that will hurt another person as a way of obtaining revenge for something the other did that made you angry is called Acting Out Anger.

Examples: John calls Mary a "bitch," and she returns this insult by slapping him in the face.

Mr. Smith and Mr. Jones are in a heated debate. Mr. Smith takes his arm and pushes all the papers and other objects on Mr. Jones' desk onto the floor.

Tom knows that Sherry does not like cigar smoke. Tom is angry at Sherry for something he hasn't mentioned to her, and when he is with her now, he tends to light up cigars.

Frank knows that it hurts and upsets his wife very much if he gets drunk. He is angry at her because he thinks she has showed too much interest in another man and soon afterwards he comes home drunk.

John knows that his parents take a great deal of pride in seeing him succeed. He has for a long time been angry at them for not accepting him for what he is, for not taking care of him better, and for downgrading any accomplishments that are not in accordance with their own tastes. He flunks out of college, which embarrasses and worries them.

Effects: Acting Out Anger can be obvious or subtle. When obvious, as for example when Mary slaps John, it usually provokes anger and a wish to retaliate on the part of the other person—that is, it makes the other person tend to act out anger also. If World War III comes and we blow ourselves up, it will be the example par excellence of Acting Out Anger as a substitute for more civilized communication.

When Acting Out Anger is subtle, both the actor and the receiver may not realize that anger is being acted out; the destructive effects are felt without anyone fully understanding the situation. For example, John may not be aware that he flunked out of school mainly to hurt his parents, and Frank may not be aware that he got drunk mainly to hurt his wife. Yet after thinking about the situation in an atmosphere which permits reflection, such as psychotherapy, for example, they may discover that Acting Out Anger was a significant motive and decide to express anger in more direct and less self-destructive ways.

Yet, for all its negative effects, Acting Out Anger occasionally brings about an at least temporary reduction in the undesired behavior of someone by punishing that behavior. For this reason it will continue to be used, even though much easier ways of settling conflicts exist.

22. *Premature Advice*

Definition: When you give advice or offer the solution to someone else's problem without first having encouraged him to talk about it and explore it freely, you are giving Premature Advice.

Examples: Jim says, "I've been bothered by this boss of mine—he keeps giving me too much work to do." Alice replies, "If I were you, I'd just tell him where to get off. I wouldn't let anybody push me around."

Lee has complained about feeling bored and unenergetic. Pat says, "What you need is some more activities! Cultivate a hobby! That'll make you feel better."

Frank has told Jane that there are some things about their relationship that he is dissatisfied with. Jane says, "Well, when my job changes in the summer, we'll start spending some more time with each other. I think that'll solve most of our problems."

Effects: Premature Advice tends to provide a false sense of closure and thereby curb the continuation of meaningful communication. Often the premature advice is incorrect, since it is not based on enough information. In our third example above, spending more time with each other might not solve Frank and Jane's problems. It could be that Frank is afraid he is not satisfying Jane sexually, and the prospect of more time together is exactly what he fears. In the first example, Jim's boss may not be making unrealistic demands;

rather, Jim may be worried about having a heart attack because he has reached the age at which his father had a heart attack. By sending advice prematurely, Alice makes it more difficult for them to explore the real issues together.

23. Indefinite Words and Phrases

Definition: People sometimes use Indefinite Words and Phrases to avoid the pain or embarrassment of speaking directly about certain events.

Examples: "I think that getting back to the other thing you were upset about is also involved with all of this we've been talking about." (As opposed to, "I think that the fact that I haven't been having orgasms is connected with your jealous feelings.")

"Where you were at on the issue of the job problem, I think, contributed to some of what we noticed about our son." (As opposed to, "I think your desire to leave the house and work was noticed by our son, and it scared him.")

Effects: This type of message is often used as a defense against the fear of openly talking about a certain topic. When this message is used with a third party, for example, a therapist or friend, it sometimes enables the two people to speak to each other without letting the third party know what they are talking about. However, unfortunately, they themselves often can't figure out what each other is talking about either. This type of message muddies the waters and confuses everybody. For it, as for Speaking about General Ways of Being, Citing Specific Behaviors and Observations is the antidote.

24. Silent Need for Nurturance

Definition: Needing some support, some "being taken care of," or some help or sympathy from another person but not asking for it is Silent Need for Nurturance.

Examples: Mary knows that John often forgets anniversaries, since he is usually so absent-minded that he doesn't know what date it is. When her birthday comes, she would like some recognition, some celebration but she feels inhibited about reminding John of her birthday. Her birthday comes, John forgets, and she feels resentful.

Fred is working on a thesis and has an advisor who is usually very critical and challenging, who often plays the "devil's advocate," and throws out criticisms that he himself does not even believe. Usually Fred is able to learn from this approach, but lately he has been feeling very discouraged about his thesis and has some problems that he doesn't know how to handle. Fred could tell the advisor, "The challenging is helpful sometimes, but I need some more supportive help at this time." Instead of asking for his support, Fred says nothing. The advisor is his usual self, and Fred goes out of the meeting resentful.

June has received much criticism from her boss and goes home feeling very upset and low. When she goes home, she looks forward to getting some support from Larry. However, she doesn't let Larry know this. He chooses this evening to let her know that he doesn't like some of the ways she has handled finances, and she is very hurt and resentful.

Mable would like Elmo to surprise her occasionally with a gift or a card, as some of her friends' husbands do. She never lets Elmo know this, and he never does it. She feels resentful and hurt.

Effects: Needing nurturance and not getting it can be very upsetting. Some of the negative emotions that result from needing nurturance and not getting it may have something to do with childhood occurrences. That is, if as a child you felt frightened that needs for nurturance would not be met, some of those unpleasant feelings may carry over into a situation in adult life, without your being aware of it. Being unloved by another adult now is not as dangerous as being unloved by your parents when you were a child, but the scariness of being unloved may still persist. It helps to be able to ask for love messages, so that you can either get them or learn that they are not coming and do something about it (that is, get used to less nurturance or get it elsewhere).

Some people think that other people should know what they need without having to ask—that if they have to ask, the gift is somehow not worth as much. The only trouble is that many times the other person does not know or forgets what his partner wants. Therefore it usually works much better if we ask for what we want. Then the other person can decide whether or not she wishes to give it. It is only by asking for what we want that we can learn what to realistically expect from others—otherwise false expectations from childhood or from other experiences may persist for a lifetime.

25. Acting Out the Need for Nurturance

Definition: Acting Out the Need for Nurturance is getting into a relatively helpless posture in order to communicate a need for help and support.

Examples: A child is walking along with his mother and tries unsuccessfully to get his mother's attention. With no obstacles in the path to make him trip, he falls down and cries. His mother responds by picking him up, holding him, and saying comforting things to him.

Frances has not received as much nurturance as she wants from Frank lately. She gets the "blues" and mopes around, and he responds by asking what's wrong, being especially nice, and watching her more attentively.

Humphrey has never asked anyone for help if he can possibly avoid it. At a time when he is under a lot of stress, he gets so drunk that he can't drive home. Some of his friends take him home and help his wife put him to bed. The friends realize that this behavior is unusual for him, and after the incident they inquire about how he's doing and suggest that he maybe ought to take it easy a little more.

Effects: Acting Out the Need for Nurturance often results in obtaining nurturance, as in the three examples above, but at the cost of getting into a helpless or unpleasant state unnecessarily.

Many people are surprised by the notion that they could "purposely" get themselves into an unpleasant situation in order to get helped out of it—that the help itself is the payoff that motivates getting into the unpleasant state. In any particular instance, the particular motive may be difficult to prove. Yet every major psychological theory of human interactions recognizes this phenomenon: the behaviorists would call the help obtained "reinforcement" for the helpless behavior; the transactional analysts would call it "getting strokes"; the social exchange theorists would say that the "outcome" of the maneuver was favorable; and the Freudians would say that "secondary gain" was obtained.

If one can ask directly for nurturance, for example by using an I Want statement, and the other can hear it, then Acting Out the Need for Nurturance is unnecessary.

26. Speaking for the Other

Definition: If I try to speak your mind for you, telling someone else what you think or feel when you are there to speak for yourself, I am preempting your efforts to define your own insights—I am Speaking for the Other.

Example: Mrs. Jones and her son Tommy, age fifteen, are talking with a therapist. Without having asked Tommy about his week, Mrs. Jones says, "I don't think Tommy's been doing too well this week. He's been going around the house like he's kind of spacy. I think what he needs is to get out and get more exercise and to find a girlfriend. What do you think, doctor?"

Effects: When Tommy hears himself spoken about in this way, as if he weren't there, he is getting several messages. One is that his own opinions about himself don't matter very much, since his mother doesn't consult him or allow him to present his ideas. Another message is that his mother thinks he should not be in control of himself: the doctor and his mother decide what he feels like and what he should do. Another message is that he doesn't need to take care of himself and make decisions for himself, since his mother is interested in doing it for him. If he buys these messages, he tends to adopt a very passive style of being; if he doesn't buy these messages, he feels resentful of his mother.

I would want the mother instead to check out each of her four assumptions with Tommy, not the doctor, or, even more preferably, to encourage and support Tommy's own statement of whatever he thinks is most important.

Exercise 11
Labeling Transactions

Each of the statements below is an example of one of the following:

Unnecessary Apologizing and Self-Effacing
Excessive Speaking about External Events
Assuming from Nonverbal Cues Rather than Checking
Silent Resentment
Acting Out Anger
Premature Advice
Indefinite Words and Phrases
Silent Need for Nurturance
Acting Out the Need for Nurturance
Speaking for the Other

Label each message below according to one or more of the

above categories.

1. For no good reason, John has a proposal turned down at work. Then, someone else at work speaks with him about it in a very condescending tone, saying, "John, after you've been around a while, then try making proposals. Until then, don't rock the boat. That's what I suggest."

2. John, who feels that this suggestion wasn't based on knowledge, resents it, but says nothing to the man.

3. John comes home, wanting some reassurance from Phyllis, but says nothing.

4. John wears a sour look on his face and, discouraged, throws down his coat. Phyllis, seeing his sour look, assumes that he is angry at her for something but does not ask about it.

5. Later Phyllis says, "Have you thought any more about what we were talking about just before we got involved in that other conversation?"

6. John replies, "If there's a medical problem, see a doctor. If not, there's no need to do anything. That's all there is to it."

7. Phyllis replies, "The last time I made an appointment to see Dr. Black, they told me I'd have to wait two weeks to be seen. That's when I decided to call Dr. Brown. Dr. Brown couldn't see me much earlier, and I had to call his secretary back three or four times before I could even be given an appointment. Then I finally made the appointment, and I said to myself, 'I wonder if he'll keep this appointment on time?' And I wondered that all day the day I was to see him. . . ."

8. John gets extremely bored listening to this but says nothing for fear of upsetting Phyllis.

9. Phyllis sees John looking bored and sleepy and thinks that he is sleepy because she has been keeping him up

too late. She resolves to put an end to lovemaking earlier in the evening so that John can get his sleep.

10. In order to communicate this conclusion, Phyllis says, "I've been thinking some things like how rested we both are and am just wondering. . .I don't know. . . ."

11. John says, "If you're worried about rest, try taking a fifteen-minute break every evening before supper and meditate. That'll be the best thing you can do."

12. John continues, "I ran into Harry the other day who was telling me about this meditation thing. He went to get taught how to do it, and they told him to bring four fruits and a handkerchief. So he said to himself, 'Where am I going to get a handkerchief this time of night?' See, he'd forgotten about the whole thing right up until about six-thirty, and it was going to start at seven o'clock. . . ."

13. Phyllis says, "I wonder if meditation would help some of the other things that we've thought about from time to time . . . ."

14. John says, "Just try it if you're interested, and don't do it if not. It's as simple as that."

15. Phyllis doesn't like the fact that "John sees everything as so pat—as black-or-white"—and thinks this to herself but says nothing.

16. Phyllis, angry, gets up and walks out of the room and slams the door.

17. John sees Phyllis looking angry and assumes that she doesn't like the idea of learning to meditate.

18. John, a few minutes later, walks into the room where she is and says, "Oh, well, all this new stuff is kind of hokey anyway."

19. Phyllis sees the disapproving look on his face and assumes that the "new stuff" he was talking about was not meditation but the new drapes that she bought today, since John is looking in that direction.

20. Phyllis, hurt by what she thinks is his disapproval of the drapes, says, "I'm sorry, Honey. . . . Sometimes I just don't think I can do anything right."
21. Phyllis wants some help and nurturance from John, and in order to communicate this, she says nothing more but cries and beats her forehead with her hand.
22. John sees that she is feeling bad and assumes she is feeling sick.
23. John says, "Why don't you go take an enema, Phyllis? That'll make you feel better."
24. Phyllis sobs bitterly, saying nothing, feeling both angry and in need of support.
25. John, unable to see her cry, says, "I'm sorry, Phyllis. I didn't mean to upset you. I just don't think sometimes; I'm sorry."
26. John continues, "Why don't you get a new dress tonight? It'll cheer you up."
27. Their son Terry comes into the room, and John says, "Terry, your mother is upset and wants you to leave her alone!"

As this story ends, Phyllis and Terry meet in the kitchen and conspire to get back at John.

Answers to Exercise 11

1. Premature Advice
2. Silent Resentment
3. Silent Need for Nurturance
4. Assuming from Nonverbal Cues Rather than Checking Out on Phyllis's part; Acting Out the Need for Nurturance on John's part
5. Indefinite Words and Phrases
6. Premature Advice
7. Excessive Speaking about External Events
8. Silent Resentment
9. Assuming from Nonverbal Cues Rather than Checking

10. Indefinite Words and Phrases
11. Premature Advice
12. Excessive Speaking about External Events
13. Indefinite Words and Phrases
14. Premature Advice
15. Silent Resentment
16. Acting Out Anger
17. Assuming from Nonverbal Cues Rather than Checking
18. Indefinite Words and Phrases
19. Assuming from Nonverbal Cues Rather than Checking
20. Unnecessary Apologizing and Self-Effacing
21. Acting Out the Need for Nurturance
22. Assuming from Nonverbal Cues Rather than Checking
23. Premature Advice
24. Silent Resentment, Silent Need for Nurturance
25. Unnecessary Apologizing and Self-Effacing
26. Premature Advice
27. Speaking for the Other

Exercise 12
Thinking up Examples of Obstructive Messages

Make up two or three examples of each of the following obstructive messages. Recall examples you've seen in the past. What were the effects?

Unnecessary Apologizing and Self-Effacing
Excessive Speaking about External Events
Assuming from Nonverbal Cues Rather than Checking
Silent Resentment
Acting Out Anger
Premature Advice
Indefinite Words and Phrases
Silent Need for Nurturance
Acting Out the Need for Nurturance
Speaking for the Other

5 Exercises: Breaking Free of Attacking and Defending

Exercise 13
Ways of Expressing Wants and Feelings

Wants and feelings are the basic stuff of communication and problem solving. Perhaps the most fundamental skill in problem solving is choosing to express these wants and feelings in ways that promote negotiation rather than defense and counterattack.

The purpose of this exercise is to heighten your awareness of the options open to you in expressing wants and feelings. I have listed below fifteen hypothetical situations in which you want the other person to do something differently. First, imagine expressing your wants and feelings by the obstructive messages—Put-Down Question and You Are Bad or You Did Something Bad. Then practice expressing the same wants and feelings through facilitative messages: use an I Feel statement, Listing Options and Choosing among Them, and an I Want statement.

Example: You are a woman. A male co-worker calls you "honey" all the time; you don't like this.

Put-Down Question: "What makes you think I'm your honey?"

You Are Bad: "You're a male chauvinist pig."

I Feel: "It irritates me when you call me 'honey'."

Listing and Choosing: "We have a problem. You call me 'honey,' and I don't like being called 'honey.' Can we discuss some options in solving this problem?"

I Want: "I'd like you to call me by my first name rather than call me 'honey,' please."

Make up a similar set of five responses and imagine yourself saying them in each of the following situations.

1. A neighbor wants to borrow something very valuable from you, but you have had to remind him several times in the past to return other things, and it was very irritating.
2. A friend of yours does not bathe enough and has an offensive odor.
3. Someone in the apartment next door is playing the piano very loudly and it bothers you.
4. Your spouse has promised to do some work on the house and hasn't done it yet.
5. You are trying to finish a job, and your boss keeps repeatedly asking you if you have finished it. His continual asking is interfering with your work.
6. Your spouse is ignoring you more than you'd like.
7. Your aunt changes the subject too often for your preferences.
8. Your child has left some jelly spilled on the kitchen counter.
9. You expect calls in the evening frequently, and your teen-age son stays on the telephone for a long time.
10. One of your co-workers walks into your office without knocking. This bothers you.
11. You are on the telephone, and the person you are talking to is very wordy. You want her to answer some questions and finish the conversation quickly.
12. Your spouse drinks more than you like.
13. Your spouse nags you too much about drinking.

14. Your employee comes in late too often.
15. A co-worker talks to you about his personal problems and keeps you from working.

Exercise 14
Persisting with Wants and Feelings
Despite Attacks and Arguments

Once you have expressed wants and feelings in facilitative messages, the next task is continuing to keep the conversation in a negotiation-oriented mode, even if the other person gives arguments and attacks that can sidetrack the discussion. One very useful skill is that of Agreeing with Part of the Criticism or Argument and then restating your want or feeling as a facilitative message.

Example:

She: "I'd like you to turn the record player down a little, please."

He: "You're one to complain about noise, with that vacuum cleaner of yours that you use."

She: "That's true, it is noisy. But I'd still like the record player turned down, please."

He: "But this isn't loud. My goodness, don't you remember how loud Freddie plays his record player?"

She: "You're right. He does play it louder. But I still am bothered when you play it this loud."

He: "I think you're pretty selfish."

She: "It could be that I am. Can we figure out what options we have to solve the problem?"

In the following exercises, practice responding to each of the listed arguments by Agreeing with Part of a Criticism or Argument, and then assertively repeating what you want. Sample answers are given after the exercises.

1. You have refused to lend some money to someone who

wants to borrow a large sum.

   A. "But you know I'd lend it to you if I were in your place."

   B. "What kind of a friend are you?"

   C. "You've gotten to be quite a miser, haven't you?"

   D. "I'll pay you back within three weeks. I promise you."

   E. "Don't you remember that time I lent you a cup of sugar?"

   F. "I thought you were a generous person."

   G. "What would it be like if everybody were like you?"

   H. "If you don't lend me this money, I'll have to sell my Cadillac!"

2. You have asked someone to knock before coming into your office.

   A. "But I let people come into my office without knocking."

   B. "What is it with you, are you paranoid?"

   C. "I didn't think you were so uptight."

   D. "I was just raised in an open environment, where people don't have artificial barriers, and got out of the habit of knocking."

   E. "Oh, don't be so finicky."

Some Possible Answers to Exercise 14

1. A. "I'm glad you would lend it to me, but I'm sorry that I don't want to lend it to you."

   B. "I could be a better friend—that's true—but I don't want to lend it."

   C. "Maybe it is miserly, but I just don't want to lend it."

   D. "I'm glad you'd be able to pay it back then, but I just don't want to lend it."

   E. "You did lend me a cup of sugar, but I just don't want to lend you the thousand dollars."

   F. "I could be a lot more generous, that's true. But I

don't want to lend it."

G. "You're right. If everybody were like me, there might be problems. But I still don't want to lend the money."

H. "My not lending you the money is causing you to sacrifice—that's true—but I don't want to lend it."

2. A. "You do. I remember that. But I'd rather that you knocked first."

B. "You could call it paranoid, I guess. I just want people to knock first."

C. "Maybe it is an example of uptightness, but I still prefer that you knock."

D. "The barriers are artificial to some extent, but I still want them to be there to the extent that you knock."

E. "It is a little finicky, I suppose, but I still want it."

Exercise 15
Using Role Playing to Practice
Agreeing with Part of a Criticism or Argument

Two people are needed for this exercise. Use the situations in Exercise 13 for practice. Use a facilitative message to express the want or feeling you have. The other person then attempts to sidetrack the conversation by Attacking with New Issues, making You Did Bad statements, asking Put-Down Questions, and giving other arguments and criticisms. Your job is to agree with part of the argument and persist with the want or feeling.

Exercise 16
Expanding Your Repertoire of Responses
to Criticism and Arguments

It is great to have Agreeing with Part of a Criticism or Argument in your repertoire of messages as an antidote to a constant need for Defending Oneself. But other ways of responding to criticism can be valuable instead of or in addition to Agreeing.

When the criticism does not give me a clear idea of what is wanted and why, I want to Ask for Specific Criticism. When I want to make sure I got the message and let the other person know I did, I use a Reflection. When I have feelings about the criticism that I want to express, I use an I Feel statement. When I want to make my wants clear and negotiate an exchange of wants, I use an I Want or Bargaining statement.

For each of the criticisms below, imagine yourself responding with each of the facilitative formats I have just mentioned.

Example: "You don't have any sense."

Responses:

A.   Agreeing with Part of a Criticism: "I could have more sense than I have."
B.   Asking for Specific Criticism: "What have I done that you thought was stupid?"
C.   Reflection: "It sounds like you're pretty disgusted with me."
D.   I Feel: "When you say that, it hurts me."
E.   Bargaining: "I want to listen to what you want from me, but in return I'd like you to be patient."

Imagine responding to each of these criticisms, using:

    A. Agreeing with Part of a Criticism or Argument
    B. Asking for More Specific Criticism
    C. Reflection
    D. I Feel
    E. I Want or Bargaining

Sample answers are provided for the first five of these.

  1.   "I think you're just saying that to build yourself up."

2. "It seemed to me like you were acting totally irresponsible."
3. "It strikes me that you're totally unwilling to work on this responsibly."
4. "I think you're just coming here and playing a game."
5. "You have no right to say something like that without even thinking about it, just off the top of your head."
6. "I think you are just saying that purposely to irritate me."
7. "You seemed to be a totally unfeeling person."
8. "I don't like the way you look today."
9. "You look wrung out."
10. "You're getting angry."
11. "You're losing control—don't lose control."
12. "It makes me very angry when you do that."
13. "You must not care about our daughter, or you wouldn't be like you are."
14. "How could you be so insensitive?"
15. "Why don't you watch out for someone besides yourself once in a while?"
16. "There you go again. You're overreacting, just like you always do."
17. "I hate you."
18. "I just can't handle it when you act like such a jerk."
19. "I think you're just saying that to cover up your own insecurity."
20. "You should be more considerate."
21. "Don't you ever say anything like that to me, ever again."
22. "If that's the way you feel about it, just get out of my life—leave!"
23. "You're the one who caused the whole problem because you're the one who left me. I didn't leave you."
24. "You're changing the subject—you're muddying the whole issue."
25. "You're being too indefinite. You talk of this, and that,

and it isn't clear at all."

26. "How can you sit there eating potato chips when you just got through saying you wanted to get in shape? That really turns me off."

27. "What do you mean by flirting like you did? What are you trying to do?"

28. "Don't use these stupid communication tricks they taught you on me. You sound so artificial—it's not you."

29. "I can't stand that sniveling, weak tone of voice you have."

Sample Answers to Exercise 16

1. A. "I could use a little building up right now, I guess. Maybe that did have something to do with my saying that." (Agreeing)

   B. "What didn't you like about my trying to build myself up?" (Asking for Specific Criticism)

   C. "You didn't like my saying that, huh?" (Reflection)

   D. "I feel embarrassed to hear you say that." (I Feel)

   E. "I'd like to be able to build myself up and have you help me do it." (I Want)

2. A. "Perhaps I could have been more conscientious."

   B. "What's the main thing that bothered you about the way I did it?"

   C. "It frightened you that the job wasn't done carefully enough?"

   D. "I feel guilty when you point that out."

   E. "I want to do it again—and for you to tell me if I do it right this time."

3. A. "Maybe I haven't communicated to you as much willingness to work as you would like to have seen."

   B. "What sort of a sign that I am willing to work on it would you like?"

   C. "Your perception is that I don't care anything about it?"

D. "When you said that, I felt angry."

E. "I want to work on it, and I want you to recognize it when I do work on it."

4. A. "There might be some 'gaminess' that I'm not aware of."

B. "What did I do that led you to see me as playing games?"

C. "You sound pretty disgusted with me."

D. "When you say that, it hurts me."

E. "I want you to tell me whenever I do anything that you see as game playing, and if you do, I'll take a look at it."

5. A. "I could have thought about it longer. That's for sure."

B. "What was it about what I said that bothers you?"

C. "You sound angry with me."

D. "When you say that, it concerns me."

E. "I want to think about what I say, but I also want you to tolerate it when I don't think sometimes."

Exercise 17
Responding to Criticism:
Translating John's and Linda's Messages

For this exercise I have engaged John and Linda to demonstrate for us how not to respond to criticism, that is, by defense and counterattack. I suggest going through this conversation three times. The first time, identify and label the messages that each uses in each numbered response. The second time through, imagine that you are Linda, and substitute for each of her statements the same five facilitative ways of responding to criticism that I have provided in the two previous exercises. The third time through, imagine that you are John, and do the same with his statements. Use:

A. Agreeing with Part of a Criticism or Argument

B. Asking for More Specific Criticism

C. Reflection

D. I Feel

E. I Want or Bargaining

Answers are provided for the first three numbered statements of each speaker.

Situation: John walks into the living room, where Linda sits reading the paper. Some things are on the floor and on the table nearby. John says, "Look at this room! You are such a slob, I don't believe it."

1. Linda replies, "Well, why don't you clean it up if you don't like it?"

2. John replies, "Why should I clean it up when I never made the mess in the first place? You are just spoiled rotten."

3. Linda replies, "You are one to be calling me spoiled when you get so upset over just a few things on the floor. You just want a mother to take care of you."

4. John replies, "Yeah, well if I want a mother, it sure wouldn't be one like your mother. I think that's where you learned to be so bossy."

5. Linda replies, "Don't you talk that way about my mother. She's got more guts than you'll ever have."

6. John replies, "Blood and guts, that's for sure. She reminds me of an army sergeant."

7. Linda replies, "You think you're really cute, don't you. You are just so cute. You'll have me split my sides laughing."

8. John replies, "Well, you're one to be talking about being cute, sitting there in those rollers. You spoil my appetite."

9. Linda replies, "Nothing could spoil your appetite, John. You're already so fat that I hear kids make jokes about you every time we go out."

10. John replies, "Yeah, well why don't you just go play with them the next time? You're about as mature as they are."

11. Linda replies, "I think I will go play with them, if it will relieve me of your company," and walks out of the room. (The story ends here, for the time being.)

Answers to Exercise 17
Labeling (first time through)

1. Put-Down Question
2. Put-Down Question, You Are Bad, Defending Oneself, Speaking about General Ways of Being
3. You Are Bad
4. Attacking with a New Issue, Speaking about General Ways of Being
5. Commanding, Defending Oneself, You Are Bad
6. Sarcasm
7. Sarcasm
8. Attacking with a New Issue, You Did Something Bad
9. You Are Bad, Attacking with a New Issue
10. Put-Down Question, You Are Bad, Speaking about General Ways of Being
11. Communication Cutoff, Acting Out Anger

Answers to Exercise 17
Translating for Linda (second time through)

1. A. "The room is kind of sloppy, isn't it?"
   B. "What about the room bothers you the most—just the things on the floor or anything else?"
   C. "You sound pretty exasperated with me."
   D. "It hurts when you call me a slob."
   E. "I'd like to do a better job cleaning up, but I'd also like you to do part. Can we make a deal about that?"
3. A. "In some ways I guess I am spoiled."
   B. "Is there anything else that I'm doing that seems spoiled to you, other than the room cleaning?"
   C. "It bothers you when I don't have my things off the floor, huh?"

D. "When you insist that everything be picked up all the time, it makes it hard for me to relax."

E. "I'd like to be able to have things messy for a while, as long as I agree to pick things up at least once a day. Is that a fair bargain?"

5. A. "I am bossy at times, aren't I?"

B. "What particular bossy things that I've done are you thinking of now?"

C. "It sounds like some of the things you don't like about my mother you also see in me, huh?"

D. "When I hear you bring up my mother, I start feeling very defensive."

E. "I want us to keep talking about our relationship and postpone bringing my mother into it for now. OK?"

Answers to Exercise 17
Translating for John (third time through)

2. A. "You've got a point; I'm criticizing you, but I'm not doing anything myself either, am I?"

B. "How often and how much would you like me to clean it up?"

C. "I see it irritates you when I don't clean up the room and expect you to do it."

D. "When you ask me to clean up items that you left around the room, though, I feel put upon and taken advantage of."

E. "I'd like you to clean up the items that you leave on the floor and also to do all the vacuuming and dusting in return for my doing the grass cutting and yard work. Is that a fair deal?"

4. A. "Yes, I do like to be taken care of at times."

B. "In what particular ways don't you want to take care of me?"

C. "You feel that I am asking too much of you?"

D. "When you say that I just want a mother, it hurts

me, because I don't see myself as just wanting to be taken care of."

E. "If you'll take care of me by cleaning this room up more often, I'd be willing to take care of you in some way that you think of. Can we figure out something?"

6. A. "There are times when I could have more guts, that's for sure."

B. "When you imply that I don't have enough guts, what particular things are you talking about that you would have liked me to do?"

C. "You're saying that I've not had enough guts to do some things you'd like me to have done?"

D. "When you say that, it hurts me and also tends to turn me against your mother."

E. "If you'll let me know what things you'd like me to do that take guts, I'll stop talking about your mother."

Exercise 18
Translating for Frank and Alice
on the Issue of Jealousy

In the following dialogue Frank and Alice attack the other and defend themselves. Go through this exercise twice. The first time, imagine that you are Alice and translate her obstructive messages into facilitative ones. The second time, be Frank and translate his obstructive messages into facilitative ones. I have suggested a facilitative message to use for each; you may compare the ones you make up with those supplied in the answers.

Situation: Frank and Alice have just come home from a party. Alice is upset because Frank paid so much attention to Betty.

1. Alice says, "Well, did you have a good time at the party looking at Betty the whole time?" (Translate this Put-

Down Question into an I Feel statement.)

2. Frank replies, "Oh no, are you going to start this again?" (Substitute for this Put-Down Question a Reflection.)

3. Alice replies, "Don't go trying to get out of it. I saw you ogling her, and you wouldn't even give me the time of day." (Translate this Command and You Are Bad statement into an I Want statement.)

4. Frank replies, "I wasn't either ogling her. You just think I'm ogling her because of your own insecurity." (Translate this Defending Oneself and You Did Something Bad statement into an I Feel statement.)

5. Alice replies, "Me insecure? You're a fine one to be talking. You're one of the most insecure people I know." (Instead of this Defending Oneself and You Are Bad and Speaking About General Ways of Being, substitute Agreeing with Part of a Criticism and I Want.)

6. Frank replies, "You should go get your head shrunk." (Substitute for this You Should statement a Reflection of Feelings.)

7. Frank continues, "You're crazy. Nobody in her right mind would get so jealous over nothing, like you do." (Translate this You Are Bad and Speaking about General Ways of Being into an I Want or Bargaining statement.)

8. Alice replies, "I'm the one that's crazy, huh? Who was it last week that was crying on my shoulder over what your boss told you at work?" (Translate this Put-Down Question and Attacking with a New Issue to Agreeing with Part of a Criticism and an I Want statement.)

9. Frank replies, "You have no right to start bringing that up at a time like this!" (Translate this You Should statement into an I Feel statement and an I Want statement.)

10. Frank continues, "I wasn't all that upset over that thing the boss said anyway, and if I'd known you were going to use the whole thing against me, I would have just

kept quiet. Or maybe what I should do is to go to somebody else if I can't trust you." (Translate this Defending Oneself, You Did Bad, and Threatening to an Agreeing with Part of a Criticism.)

11. Alice replies, "Go ahead and go to somebody else. It wouldn't bother me one bit." (Translate this into an I Feel statement accurately portraying Alice's reaction to what Frank has just said.)

12. Alice continues and bursts into tears and says, "And you would go to somebody else, too. I know you would!" (Translate this You Are Bad statement into a Reflection of the feelings behind Frank's threat.)

13. Frank replies, "Let's just not talk about it anymore, OK? I can't take any more of this." (Translate this Communication Cutoff into a Reflection of Feelings.)

14. Alice replies, "You never did want to get married in the first place. I know you didn't." (Translate this You Did Bad statement and Attacking with a New Issue into a Reflection of Feelings responding to what Frank has just said.)

15. Frank replies, "Oh shut up! You're just trying to get sympathy by blubbering like you always do." (Substitute for this Command and You Did Something Bad statement a Reflection showing empathy for what Alice has just said.)

16. Alice says, "You're so insensitive and callous. I can't believe it." (Translate this You Are Bad and Speaking about General Ways of Being into Agreeing with Some Part of a Criticism or an I Want statement.)

17. Frank walks out, as our story ends.

Some Possible Answers to Exercise 18
Translating for Alice (first time through)

1. "Frank, when we were at the party and I noticed you looking at Betty, it made me feel hurt because I had the

idea you were more interested in her than in me."

3. "When we go to parties, I want you to pay more attention to me and less attention to other women."

5. "Maybe it is because of my insecurity, but I'd still like you to spend more time and attention with me rather than with the other women."

8. "Maybe it is because I'm crazy, but I still want you to spend more time with me at these parties."

11. "When you mentioned going to somebody else, that scared me and made me start to feel less close to you to keep from being so scared."

12. "I have the idea, or the hope, that you wouldn't really go to somebody else, or not another woman, but that you were saying that because I made you mad. Is that right?"

14. "I guess this conversation has been pretty hard on you, just like it has for me, huh Frank?"

16. "Maybe I am blubbering because I want sympathy. I probably am. I guess I just generally want more support and love from you than I'm getting, Frank."

Some Possible Answers to Exercise 18
Translating for Frank (second time through)

2. "Are you saying you would have liked me to pay more attention to you than I did?"

4. "When you say that I was ogling her, I feel upset and frustrated because I don't like giving you those jealous feelings."

6. "I guess I've made you mad at me, first by looking at Betty and then by calling you insecure just then."

7. "Someday I would like you to try to get to where you can tolerate my looking at other women. If I work on looking at them less and paying more attention to you at parties, will you work on getting more secure with my looking around?"

9. "When you bring up that issue about my boss, it makes me hurt and angry. I'd like us to finish first with talking about the party and then to talk about that incident afterwards."

10. "But you're right. What the boss said to me hurt me, and I have some insecurities myself, all right."

13. "Sounds like I upset you and made you mad when I said that about going to someone else. Is that right?"

15. "It sounds like you're saying you never have gotten the support and love from me that you've wanted, even from the time we first got married. Is that right?"

Exercise 19
Responding with Facilitative Messages
While Being Blasted for a Mistake

Everyone makes mistakes, and sometimes they are costly to someone else. If that someone else is very angry and accusing, it is very difficult to respond with facilitative messages. The tendency is to respond with Defending Oneself and Attacking with a New Issue, and You Did Something Bad statements, on the one hand, or else with Unnecessary Apologizing and Self-Effacing, on the other hand.

In the following exercise Jill responds with facilitative messages to the blasts of John. Imagine yourself as Jill and respond to each of John's messages. Compare your response with hers. The second time through, identify the types of messages each uses. Answers are provided.

Situation: John is Jill's boss; she is his secretary. John walks in carrying a file folder.

1. John says, "Why can't you do things right? What in the world are you thinking of?"

2. Jill replies, "What is it that I've done that wasn't right?" (Jill looks John in the eye, sits up straight, and has an information-seeking tone of voice.)

3. John throws the folder down on her desk and says, "Do you need me to tell you what you've done? Can you see this or can't you?"

4. Jill looks at the folder and sees that it is one that John had asked her about earlier in the day. Jill says, "Did I make a mistake about this folder?"

5. John mimics her voice in a very uncomplimentary tone, saying, " 'Did I make a mistake about this folder?' No, you didn't make a mistake, I'm just standing here passing the time of day, that's all. Of course you made a mistake! You told me this file wasn't in the file cabinet, and I looked all over everywhere for it, and then finally I come in and find it in the filing cabinet, just at the right place! Just where you told me it wasn't!"

6. Jill replies, "Looks like I blew it, didn't I? I feel bad about costing you time like that." (Jill says this in a sincere tone of voice, communicating that she does feel bad somewhat, but nevertheless her tone is still forthright and self-accepting, communicating that she thinks she's OK even though she's made a mistake.)

7. John says, "You might say you blew it. You just might say that. What were you thinking of? It was right there in plain sight!"

8. Jill says, "You're pretty mad at me about this, aren't you?"

9. John says, "No, I'm not mad. I like spending time looking all around for something that is right in the file cabinet where it should be. I like putting off pressing matters while I do that. I've got a deadline to meet on Wednesday, you know."

10. Jill says, "Can you think of any ways I can undo some of the damage I've caused and help you meet your deadline quicker?"

11. John says, "No, just stay out of it. You'd only slow me down."

12. Jill says, "When I hear you say that, I feel bad. I'd like

to help you out. I don't think that beating myself over the head about it would help anything, so I don't intend to do that. I do intend to look for files more carefully in the future, and I'd like to help you out with your deadline if you will let me."

13. John says, "Well just don't let it happen again if you want to keep your job." He walks out.

This story ends by Jill following through with her intention not to punish herself nonproductively. She mentally rehearses looking more carefully for files and then goes back to work on some other things. Later on, John comes back into the office, apologizes profusely for losing his temper, praises her for the good work that she generally has done, and asks her to do something on his project.

Answers to Exercise 19

1. Put-Down Question
2. Asking for Specific Criticism
3. Put-Down Question
4. Asking for Specific Criticism
5. Sarcasm, You Did Something Bad
6. Agreeing with Part of Criticism, I Feel or Self-Disclosure
7. Sarcasm, Put-Down Question
8. Reflection of Feelings
9. Sarcasm
10. Asking for Specific Criticism (in other words, she is asking him what he wants now)
11. Commanding, You Did Bad
12. I Feel, I Want, I Intend, I Want
13. Threatening

6 Exercises: Listing Options and Choosing Among Them

Exercise 20 A Fantasy Exercise
Proposing the Method of
Listing and Choosing to Another Person

In each of the situations below, Bill or Mary makes an obstructive beginning to the discussion of the problem. In your fantasy, start the discussion differently by proposing and beginning Listing Options and Choosing among Them.

Before you list options, it is best if both of you carry out these tasks: (1) At least one of you states what it is that you each want in as neutral and value-free terms as possible. (2) This person asks whether or not he agrees with this view of the problem. (3) The second person makes a Reflection of the first person's view of the problem. (4) If the second person has a different view of the problem, he states it. When both agree on what the problem is, then (5) one of you suggests Listing Options, and if the other consents, then start listing.

This pattern, of course, is a guide, a model, that does not have to be rigidly followed, just as is everything else suggested in this book. But in the fantasy exercises, imagine yourself going through these five introductory steps on each of the following problems. Sample answers are listed after the exercises.

Situation 1

Bill, upon getting home from work, is almost always tired and wants to relax and watch TV. Mary, on the other hand, is bored and wants to go out and visit, etc. They often argue over this.

Mary says, "We never go out. We never do anything. Can't you ever get excited over anything? You're a vegetable in the evenings." (Instead of these Put-Down Questions and You Are Bad statements, introduce Listing Options and Choosing among Them.)

Situation 2

Mary is rather frugal and is concerned that Bill is spending too much money. Bill is contemplating another big purchase, a car, to be made with money which belongs to the two of them.

Mary says nothing. Bill buys the car, and Mary silently resents. (In place of Silent Resentment, substitute the method of problem solving by Listing Options and Choosing among Them.)

Situation 3

Bill wants to know where Mary is and when to expect her to be back home, but Mary is not as attentive to time as Bill is. It fairly frequently happens that Mary comes home late to find an irate Bill, and they fight. In these fights Bill asserts his desire to be notified of Mary's plans and wants her to show up on time. Mary wants to do this but finds it difficult to remember.

Bill says, "If this lateness keeps up, you are going to find out that you have no one to come home to. I'm not standing for it." (For these threats substitute Listing Options and Choosing among Them.)

Situation 4

Mary has to be at work at 7:30 in the morning. Bill does not have to be at work until 9:00. Consequently, she gets up earlier in the morning, while he continues to sleep. The plan then is for Mary to wake Bill up just before she leaves for work. However, sometimes Bill says "OK" but then falls back to sleep, and sometimes Mary forgets to wake him up. When Bill is late to work, they invariably argue over whose fault it is.

Mary says to herself, "I will take the blame every time just to avoid these fights." (In place of this Silent Resentment, substitute the method of problem solving by Listing Options and Choosing among Them.)

Situation 5

Mary is a much neater person than Bill is. They have divided up the housekeeping chores so that they are both supposed to do an equal amount of cleaning up. However, Bill often postpones cleaning up, and Mary in the meantime either does the cleaning herself and feels resentful toward Bill or else waits for Bill to do it, feeling irritated by the sight of messiness until it is done. Mary sometimes mentions the messiness to Bill. When this happens, Bill agrees to do the cleaning, apologizing profusely for not having done it, and sometimes does it conscientiously for a day or two, then goes back into the former pattern. The two of them also share other chores equally, such as cooking, food buying, doing laundry, etc., and Bill is rather conscientious at these duties.

(Mary and Bill are visiting another couple.) Mary says, "You know, this is the cleanest place you've got here; I wish our place could be kept so clean and neat." (In place of this Expressing Dissatisfaction through a Third Party, substitute the method of problem solving through Listing Options and Choosing among Them.)

Situation 6

Mary is in the habit of listening to music played very loudly. This bothers Bill, who likes to read in silence. Bill sometimes suffers without saying anything and finds that he feels resentful toward Mary for the disturbance. At other times Bill asks Mary to turn the music down, which she does, but then she feels a little resentful toward Bill.

Bill says, "I'm not going to put up with any more loud music, and that's all there is to it. If you want to listen to it loud enough to blast your ears out, you can go get yourself some earphones. Why didn't you already do that, anyway, seeing how much it bothers me—didn't you think of it?" (Replace this Command and Put-Down Question with the method of problem solving by Listing Options and Choosing among Them.)

Situation 7

Mary smokes, and cigarette smoke bothers Bill very much. When Mary has smoked, Bill has made comments like "God, you've had three of those just since we've been sitting here," or "Are you going to smoke another one already?" indicating rather indirectly that he doesn't like the smoke. Mary usually smokes anyway, and the two feel resentful toward each other.

Bill says nothing and silently feels resentful. Later, at a party, the topic of smoking comes up, and Bill says, in Mary's presence, "Mary here makes the house smell like rotten eggs with these damn cigarettes. It makes me want to puke whenever I walk inside." (Replace this Expressing Dissatisfaction through a Third Party and You Are Bad statement with the method of problem solving by Listing Options and Choosing among Them.)

Situation 8

Mary is in the habit of sitting in the living room and reading. Bill, who doesn't get to see Mary as much as he would like, is in the habit of going into the living room and asking Mary questions, trying to start a conversation. Sometimes Mary gets into the conversation, but most of the time she feels resentful toward Bill for interrupting when she is trying to think about the reading. So she responds to his questions in a cross and short-tempered way, saying things that make him feel that in general she is not interested in having him around.

Bill asks a question again, and Mary says, "How should I know that? Why don't you find out for yourself?" (Replace this Put-Down Question with the method of problem solving by Listing Options and Choosing among Them.)

Possible Answers to Exercise 20

Situation 1

"I've been thinking about what we like to do in the evenings. We have a problem because you want to relax and watch TV, and I want to go out and do something exciting, and I don't think either of us is comfortable with the way things are. Do you see the problem the same way?" She then allows Bill to respond, and later says, "Can we figure out what options we have and which of them we both think are worth trying?"

Situation 2

"Bill, I think we've run into the same conflict over this car that we've run into a lot before: You want to spend more and I want to save more. Is that the way you see it, too . . . ? I'd like for us to figure out what options we have and which of them we both think are worth trying."

Situation 3

"Mary, it bothers me that we waste so much energy fighting over the fact that I like you to be home on time and you often like to come in late. Do you see the problem that way, too . . . ? I hope that we can figure out some new system where we won't have to keep hassling each other over this. I'd like us to figure out what options we have and which of them we both think are worth trying."

Situation 4

"Bill, this arrangement about getting up in the mornings that we've gotten into doesn't seem to be working too well, does it? I want a way for you to be waked up every time, and you do, too, but it isn't working very well. Do you see the problem that way, too . . . ? Can we think about making a new arrangement, and figure out what options we have and which of them we both think are worth trying?"

Situation 5

"You know, Bill, this arrangement we have on the chores doesn't seem to be working very well. You are able to tolerate disorder a lot more easily than I can, so I spend a lot of time worrying about when your cleaning is going to get done, and I think you realize that and it makes you uncomfortable. Do you see it like that . . . ? I wonder if we can think about what options we have for a different arrangement and figure out what option we both think is worth trying out."

Situation 6

"Mary, I've been thinking about the situation that we have gotten into with the issue of the music. It doesn't seem to be very satisfactory to either of us. Sometimes I get you to turn it down, and sometimes I tolerate it being loud, but I'm wondering if we could figure out some general plan that might suit us both better. Do you see the problem that way, too . . . ? Can we think some about what our options are and which ones we both think are worth trying?"

Situation 7

"Mary, I've been thinking about our situation regarding your smoking. I've been getting in little digs at you, which hasn't done either of us much good. I'd like very much not to breathe cigarette smoke any more than I have to, but you don't want to quit altogether just for me. That's the conflict, isn't it . . . ? Can we figure out what options we have and which of them we both think are worth trying?"

Situation 8

"Bill, when you come in and talk to me when I'm trying to read, I get irritable. But at the same time, I really like talking with you, and I'm glad you are interested in talking with me. Do you see that conflict the same way . . . ? Can we figure out a way that when we talk I can really get into it? Let's figure out what options we have and which ones we both think are worth trying."

Exercise 21   A Fantasy or Role-Playing Exercise
Practicing Thinking of Options

When solving problems by Listing Options and Choosing among Them, you may give full vent to your creative urges and consider anything your mind can conceive. Here are some possible forms that solutions might take; this list may help you in generating options.

1. I give in totally to what you want in this situation, not expecting anything in return. (E.g., I'll stop smoking, and not even consider it a favor to you, but as something I'm doing for myself.)
2. I give in to what you want, expecting in return only that you will let me know whether or not you liked it and that if you did like it, you will acknowledge that I did you a favor and show me some gratitude. (E.g., I'll be civil to your Aunt Beulah if you will realize that it's an effort and thank me for it if I'm successful.)
3. I give in to what you want. Our plan consists of something that makes it easier for me to do it. (E.g., Bill will go out with Mary at night, and he can take a nap to make him more energetic.)
4. We compromise on this particular issue so that each of us gets partial fulfillment of our wants. (E.g., I'll turn my record player down lower than I want but higher than you want it so that we're sacrificing equally.)
5. I give in on this particular issue at this particular time in

return for a sacrifice from you at a later time. (E.g., I'll play my record player as loud as I want to tonight, and in return I won't play it so that you can hear it for the rest of the week.)

6. I give in on this particular issue for all time in return for a sacrifice from you on a different issue. (E.g., I'll tolerate your record player if you'll tolerate my long stories.)

7. We can think of a technological or other creative solution that will allow each of us to get our wants met. (E.g., We'll get some earphones with a long extension cord for the record player.)

8. For now, I can avoid the behavior you can't tolerate if you will work on being more able to tolerate it in the long run. (E.g., I'll criticize you less for now if you'll try to become less vulnerable to criticism.)

9. We will deal with another issue that seems to make this one more difficult to solve. (E.g., we'll start being more open with each other about other behaviors we like and don't like so that we won't need to channel all our resentment into the "stock" issues of the record player and the cigarette smoke.)

10. We'll agree that you will tell me whenever your wants are not being met or when you're feeling irritated regarding this issue, and at that time I'll probably do something about it. The main benefit of this agreement is that you feel free about expressing your feelings on it without worrying about hurting me or the relationship. (E.g., whenever I start telling long anecdotes that bore you, you'll feel free to tell me to cut it down.)

11. I'll give in to what you want in this situation to some degree with the expectation that sooner or later you will give in to what I want—not in a scheduled way, but whenever a time comes up. (E.g., tonight I'll go with you to the party even though I don't feel like it; maybe sometime down the road you'll go by yourself or stay home with me even though you don't feel like it.)

12. You'll do this for me in response to my doing something as yet unthought of for you. (E.g., if you'll work on speaking more distinctly for me, I'll work on changing some of my behaviors that you don't like.)

13. We can explore and redefine the meaning of the behaviors involved and establish that the behaviors are not a signal of love versus absence of love. Thus we can lessen some of the false importance of the problem. (E.g., I can let you know that my being late is a pattern I have been in since early childhood and has nothing to do with how much or little I value or love you. You, who grew up in a family where lateness was a sign of anger or not caring, can understand and tolerate my lateness better now, and I can understand and tolerate your anger better.)

Referring to the above list, if you wish, think up as many options as you can for each of the eight situations in Exercise 20. They don't have to be reasonable; a far-out suggestion might be just what is needed to bring to mind a workable alternative. If you are by yourself, simply list options in your imagination; if you are with someone else, role play the discussion and list options together. Some possible options for the first situation follow.

In Situation 1, where Bill wants to relax and watch TV in the evenings and Mary wants to go out, there are many possible options.

1. Mary can go out anyway, leaving Bill to relax; Mary would find other people to go out with in the evenings.

2. They can plan to go out together on certain evenings and stay in on others, thus giving each some degree of satisfaction.

3. Bill can arrange to get off work a little early on some days and come home and take a nap before the evening so that he will have the energy to have fun with Mary.

4. Bill can start putting tranquilizers in Mary's food. (Options like this one that are obviously facetious and unworkable are nevertheless often helpful. They loosen up the discussion and may even suggest workable options such as option 5.)

5. Mary can get an exciting job that will fulfill some of her need for excitement and leave her more interested in resting in the evenings.

6. Mary can do other activities in the daytime that meet this same need.

7. Bill can get a less draining job.

8. Bill and Mary can deal with their unexpressed hostilities to each other which have led them to "get at" each other by thwarting each other's evening plans.

9. Bill and Mary can find a couple like them so that the two couples can get together and the sleepy ones can relax and the lively ones can be lively.

10. Bill and Mary can enact scenes from *Who's Afraid of Virginia Woolf* and yell at each other at the beginning of the evening in order to get themselves perked up. (Here's another improbable option that may nevertheless cast some light on the issue. It suggests that option 8—dealing with unexpressed hostilities—may have some merit.)

11. Bill and Mary can talk about the meaning of each other's actions. They can come to realize that their respective patterns of going out or staying in are long-standing habits and not a sign that they don't love each other. With this redefinition, the conflict may be less painful.

12. Bill may go out more in the evenings. In return Mary realizes that he is sacrificing for her and lets him know she appreciates it.

Exercise 22
Identifying Immediate Problems
and More Long-Run Problems

Sometimes a certain problem poses both an immediate problem ("How are we going to handle this situation this time?") and a long-run problem ("How are we going to keep this problem from bugging us over and over?") In such cases it is beneficial for the two people to consider *both* problems and perhaps to hold two separate sessions of Listing Options and Choosing among Them.

For example, you and I both want to use the car tonight. Our first problem is, Who's going to use the car tonight? And the second problem is, How are we going to make some sort of schedule or customary way of arranging who uses the car and who doesn't, so that the problem doesn't keep repeating itself?

For a second example, you are my boss. You have made some of your work higher priority for the secretary to do than my work, yet I have a pressing need for my work to get done. Our first problem is, How do we settle the issue of this particular piece of work? and our second problem is, How do we arrange some sort of system for determining the priority of work so that a long-run solution is achieved?

Sometimes people attempting to solve problems get into trouble when one is trying to solve the immediate problem and the other is trying to solve the more long-run problem. Consider the following piece of dialogue.

1st Person: "But how do I know I'm not going to have to do this over and over again?"

2nd Person: "We've got *today* to deal with. If I don't have this today, I'll be sunk."

1st Person: "Today is just another example of what keeps happening over and over. What we do about today isn't going to change the pattern that we're in one bit."

Both of these people are right: they have two problems to solve. What they need to do is to get together and work first on the immediate problem and then on the long-range one, instead of bickering over whether the problem is immediate or long-run.

For each of the situations below, identify the immediate problem and the long-run problem. Using either role playing or fantasy, practice going through two separate problem-solving sessions on each one of them. Assume that each of these situations comes up recurrently in the relationship.

1. Your teenage daughter is on the telephone and you are awaiting a call from one of your friends.
2. You want to stay out late tonight, but your spouse, who has more of an "early to bed, early to rise" philosophy, wants to get in early.
3. An employee is conscientious, but a very poor writer. This person has written a report which you, the supervisor, think is unusable because of the quality of the writing.
4. An entire group of people waits for the completion of your work. Each of them seems to constantly bug you to find out whether it is done or not. You get a call from the boss of this group. She wants to know whether the work is ready or not.
5. An employee feels that her boss assigned a co-worker to an exciting project not because of the co-worker's ability but because of her personal relationship with the male boss.
6. A mother wants the son's room clean tonight when company comes. The son generally wants to have his own room as he likes it.
7. An employee wants some time off; the supervisor wants more advance notice.

Exercise 23
A Role-Playing Exercise

Use any of the situations listed so far or any in the Situations Catalogue of Chapter 11, or real situations in your life, and with your partner go through the entire process of Listing Options and Choosing among Them. Refer to the model below.

Step 1: Both define what they see each as wanting, in as neutral terms as possible, and check out by Reflections whether the other sees the problem in the same way. When they do, they agree to list options.

Step 2: They list options (Bargaining statements are useful).

Step 3: They evaluate options (I Want and I Feel statements are useful here).

Step 4: They agree to try one option (for a certain length of time).

Step 5: They try it.

Step 6: They talk about it again, and if it hasn't worked, they use their additional information to problem solve again.

This exercise is extremely valuable. The more it is performed, the better!

7 Sarcasm and Verbal-Nonverbal Incongruity: Making Alternatives Happen

Sarcasm and Verbal-Nonverbal Incongruity share a common aspect: the verbal message that is given is not fully meant and thus is hard to respond to; there is always a nonverbal or contextual message that disqualifies the verbal one. In order to get out of the habit of sending these messages, or to best deal with them when someone else sends them to you, the task is the same: to express, comment on, lay on the table the messages that are being sent so that they can be dealt with directly. What does each person want? The facilitative communicator pushes the conversation in this direction, not to defeat the other, but so that they might both win.

Exercise 24 A Fantasy Exercise
Translating for Oswald and Harriet

Go through the following exercise twice. The first time, imagine that you are Harriet and substitute facilitative messages for her obstructive ones. Suggested alternatives are given in parentheses. The second time, do the same for Oswald. Answers are provided after the exercise.

Situation: Harriet has just bought a very expensive dress that Oswald thinks was unnecessary.
1. Oswald says, "Well, do you think you spent enough money today, or do you want to go back and try some

more?" (Try Expressing Mixed Feelings instead of Sarcasm.)

2. Harriet replies, "You're just upset because you can't make enough money for us and jealous because of my job." (Try Reflection of Feelings, Agreeing with Part of a Criticism, and an I Want statement instead of this You Are Bad and Attacking with a New Issue.)

3. Oswald replies, "Oh, sure I'm jealous. I would just love to have your position. I would love to be chief servant to the rich people. Do you think you could get me a job?" (Try Agreeing with Part of a Criticism and an I Want statement instead of this Sarcasm.)

4. Harriet says nothing in reply, but as she rearranges the books on the table, she throws them down with loud force. (Try an I Feel statement instead of or in addition to these Nonverbal Messages.)

5. Oswald continues, "And one more thing: you are not buying anything else without my permission until we get our finances straightened out. You are taking that dress back, tomorrow!" (Oswald might try introducing Listing Options and Choosing among Them rather than these Commanding statements.)

6. Harriet replies, "Do you know what my mother told me? She said, 'No man will ever know what it takes to make a woman happy. I'd just stay away from them, if I had it to do over again.' And you know, I think she was right." (Try an I Feel statement in response to Oswald's last utterance and a Bargaining statement instead of this Overgeneralizing statement of Harriet's.)

7. Oswald replies, "With a mother like yours telling you stuff like that, it's no wonder you're so screwed up and hard to get along with." (Instead of this You Are Bad statement, try a Reflection of Feelings.)

8. Harriet replies, "Oh, yeah, listen to Mr. Perfection over there talking about getting along with people! Tell me more, professor. Just wait long enough for me to take

notes!" (Instead of this Sarcasm, try Agreeing with Part of a Criticism or Argument.)

9. Oswald replies, "You really would like to be funny, wouldn't you? Well you are, you're real funny. Don't you see how hard I'm laughing? I'm just about to split a gut, I'm laughing so hard. Have you ever thought of going on television, Harriet?" (Instead of this Sarcasm and Put-Down Questions, Oswald might try Agreeing with Part of a Criticism or Argument.)

10. Harriet replies, "I haven't thought of going on television, no, but I have thought of just going, period. I think it'd be very good for you to see what it's like without me to be sarcastic to." (Instead of this Threat, Harriet might try an I Feel statement about the whole conversation and an I Want statement about the financial issue that started the whole discussion.)

11. Oswald replies, "Oh, I'd just be lost without the sound of your sweet voice to brighten up my day." (Instead of this Sarcasm, try Agreeing with Part of a Criticism.)

12. Harriet replies, "OK, why don't I just leave right now if you'd like that so much?" (Instead of this Threat and Put-Down Question, try Agreeing with Part of a Criticism and Bargaining.)

13. Oswald replies, "You're just insecure, like everyone in your family always has been and always will be." (This statement really deserves a medal in that it combines Overgeneralizing, You Are Bad, Speaking about General Ways of Being and Attacking with a New Issue! Try substituting a Reflection of Feelings.)

14. Harriet storms out of the room, loudly pulls her suitcase out of the closet, and very vigorously starts throwing her clothes into the suitcase. (Instead of this Acting Out Anger and Need for Nurturance, Harriet might try an I Feel statement and a Communication Postponement.)

15. Oswald goes into the room and yells, "Put that stupid bag up! Can't you tell when I'm serious and when I'm

kidding?" (Instead of this Command and Put-Down Question, Oswald might try Reflection of Feelings and an I Feel statement, and offer a Communication Postponement.)

16. Harriet says nothing but continues packing. (Instead of Acting Out Anger and Need for Nurturance, Harriet might try to Reflect Oswald's last statement.)

The story ends, for the time being, in this way: Oswald kicks Harriet's bag onto the floor and throws the clothes onto the floor saying, "I love you too much to let you leave me!" Harriet flies at him, bursting into tears and sobbing, and pounds on his chest with her fists. Oswald holds her by the shoulders, and after giving her a few shakes, repeating, "I love you too much to let you leave," he pulls her to him. She resists, then gives in, and they embrace for a few seconds. He tries to kiss her, but she breaks loose and runs out the front door, as he yells after her. She returns in ten minutes, and Oswald says, "Harriet?" She replies, "Leave me alone, I don't want to talk about it." She goes into a room by herself, and he paces back and forth dramatically as the curtain falls.

Possible Answers for Exercise 24
Translating for Harriet (first time through)

2. "You're concerned about the price, aren't you? I'll admit that it is pretty expensive, but I want to get it anyway, and if you'll sit down with me, I'll show you how we can afford it."

4. "Oswald, when you're sarcastic about my job like that, it hurts me."

6. "Oswald, when you order me like that, it makes me feel rebellious and only want to spite you. Let's make a deal: I'll at least consider taking the dress back if you'll at least consider taking back that gun you bought. Let's sit down and go over the budget and decide what we can and can't afford and what we need to take back."

8. "You're right. I could be a lot easier to get along with. That's for sure."

10. "Oswald, this whole conversation is making me feel frustrated because I don't think we're getting anything accomplished. I really want us to figure out something about this financial issue that we can at least try. I would like us to list our options and choose among them."

12. "I'm sure my sarcasm must get on your nerves. Let's make a deal: if I'll try to be less sarcastic and more straight with you, will you do the same thing? And can we both try it out right now when we go over our finances?"

14. "Oswald, I'm feeling more and more upset, and when you mentioned my family, I got even more upset. I think I'm too upset to talk very productively with you right now. I'd like to go out and walk around for about half an hour and then start back and see if we can do better the second time, OK?"

16. "Oswald, are you saying that you didn't fully mean all the things you said in the last few minutes?"

Translation for Oswald (second time through)

1. "Harriet, that's a pretty dress, and I like it, but at the same time I'm concerned that we may not be able to pay our bills this month if you buy it. Can we talk about that some?"

3. "You're right that I don't make as much money as I'd like to. It could be that I may be jealous about your job, too—I don't know, I'll have to think about that one some. But whether or not, I want us to sit down and make sure we can pay our water bill before you buy an expensive dress."

5. "Harriet, I think we have a problem: each of us isn't satisfied with the way the other handles money. I'd like us to take some time and figure out what our options

are regarding how we make decisions on expenditures and then see if there's an option that we can both agree to try. OK?"

7. "Sounds like I haven't been making you happy too much, Harriet."

9. "You're right, I'm not such a great one to be talking, am I? I could certainly stand to improve how I get along with you, couldn't I?"

11. "It would be hard on me if you left. You're right about that."

13. "It sounds like you're pretty fed up and disgusted with the way I run my mouth."

15. "Harriet, it looks like I've really upset you, and I've gotten upset myself. Let's both take a few minutes to get ourselves back together, and then I think we'll both be able to be more reasonable. OK?"

Exercise 25
Responding Facilitatively to
Sarcasm and Verbal-Nonverbal Incongruity

In this situation, Michael and Richard are co-workers at the same level. Michael is a very hard-working person who is interested in a promotion; Richard has been at the job longer and wants the promotion also. Richard has resented Michael and has showed this resentment in various ways. Michael decides to talk with Richard about the situation. He meets much obstructive communication, but carries on.

Imagine yourself as Michael and respond to each of Richard's messages. Your goal is to improve relations with Richard, if possible, but at any rate to have his resentment be something that is "on the table" rather than going on behind your back.

The second time through, identify the messages. Answers to these are provided.

1. Michael says, "Richard, I'd like to talk to you a little bit about your attitude toward my being here and the work I'm doing. I've been getting some signs that you resent me, and I want us to at least talk about it."

2. Richard looks at Michael with a very hostile facial expression, and says, "I don't resent you, Michael. You do whatever you want to."

3. Michael replies, "The specific things that make me think there was some resentment are that you frequently have an unfriendly look on your face when I'm around, you have avoided working with me on projects on the two or three times that I've asked you, I've gotten reports from other people that you don't like me, and the other day at the cafeteria I overheard you talking about me and calling me an ass-kisser and a power-grabber. When these things have happened, I've felt hurt and angry, and I want to talk it over with you."

4. Richard says, "You've built up quite an impressive case, haven't you, just like you do in everything else. What were you doing: eavesdropping on my table, or did you have it bugged?"

5. Michael says, "I can see how you wouldn't like the idea of having a case built up against you. But I'd like it if you didn't look at it that way, but as a chance for us to get some things out into the open, and maybe get along better because of it."

6. Richard says, "Oh sure, Michael, I'm really *sure* that you're interested in our having a good relationship. I know that's just number one on your priority list."

7. Michael says, "You're right when you imply that it's not number one on my priority list; however, I do want it. I'd like you to say whatever you don't like about me directly to me, and maybe we can reach some understanding about it."

8. Richard replies, "Michael, you're trying to get me on your side, like you try to get everybody on your side."

9. Michael says, "You don't like how I try to get people on my side? I'll admit, I really do prefer having someone on my side than not on my side. You're right about that."

10. Richard replies, "You make that very obvious, Michael."

11. Michael says, "What don't you like about the way I do that? What would you like me to do differently?" (This is spoken in a serious, enthusiastic tone, as if he really is interested in getting Richard's opinion.)

12. Richard replies, "Michael, I'm sure you can lead your life just fine without me to tell you what to do. I've got some work to do this afternoon, so if you don't mind . . . ."

13. Michael replies, "You're right, I can live my life just fine, but I'd still like to hear your opinion directly from you rather than behind my back. I feel angry that you'll talk about me but not to me."

14. Richard says, "OK then, you want to hear my opinion? I think you're constantly kissing the boss's ass and that you're constantly trying to push your way up without any regard for anybody else. I think you're totally and completely out for yourself. There, are you satisfied?"

15. "I like hearing it from you straight, like that, Richard. I don't like it that you feel that way, but at least I like hearing it straight." Michael continues, "I agree that I am out for myself. But I also want to do well by the people I work with in any way I can. So if you can think of some specific things you'd like me to change, I'd like to hear about it. OK?"

Richard says, "OK, I'll think about it," and goes back to his work as the vignette ends. Michael feels better about the situation now and figures that he'll be OK whether or not Richard changes. (Whether or not Richard will change is left to the reader's imagination.)

Answers to Exercise 25

1. Mutual Topic Finding, I Want, Reflection of Feelings
2. Verbal-Nonverbal Incongruity
3. Citing Specific Behaviors, Reflection, I Feel, I Want
4. Sarcasm, Put-Down Question
5. Reflection of Feelings, I Want statement
6. Sarcasm
7. Agreeing with Part of a Criticism, I Want
8. You Did Something Bad
9. Reflection of Feelings, Agreeing with Part of a Criticism
10. You Did Something Bad
11. Asking for Specific Criticism, Nonverbal "I'm OK, You're OK"
12. Sarcasm, Attempt at Communication Cutoff
13. Agreeing with Part of Criticism, I Want, I Feel
14. You Did Something Bad, You Are Bad, Put-Down Question
15. Expressing Mixed Feelings, Agreeing with Part of a Criticism, I Want, Asking for More Specific Criticism

Exercise 26
Responding Facilitatively to
Verbal-Nonverbal Incongruity

Some people make it unpleasant to communicate wants to them in a straightforward manner because they respond by attacking. Others make it equally unpleasant by responding with a great display of being hurt and unappreciated—the "martyr" response. In a series of messages designed to elicit guilt, they remind you of how they have greatly sacrificed and have received no gratitude, yet refuse to express anger or ask you to make it up or do anything which would equalize the unequal sacrifice they feel they have made.

In the following exercise Mark responds as a martyr when Lillian makes a request of him. Imagine yourself to be Lillian and imagine yourself responding to each comment of

Mark's. Compare your response with what Lillian says. The second time through, identify the messages used.

Situation: Mark and Lillian are co-workers. Mark is in the habit of putting his hands on Lillian when he speaks with her. He greets her, for example, and puts his arm around her and rubs her on the shoulder or on the arm or the neck while talking with her. He does this again, and Lillian brings up the matter with him.

1. Lillian says, "Mark, will you do me a favor? When you touch me and put your arm around me, I usually don't like that. I'd like you not to do that, please."

2. Mark had been smiling, but upon hearing this, his face drops. He says, "Well, certainly, I won't. I *certainly apologize.*" (These words spoken in a very offended, martyrish tone.)

3. Lillian says, "How do you feel about my saying that, Mark?"

4. Mark replies, "No, it's OK. I don't mind at all. I was just trying to be friendly, but obviously you don't like my kind of friendliness. It's quite all right." (Mark says this in a very hurt and self-pitying tone of voice.)

5. Lillian says, "I like your friendliness. I just don't like it when you touch me. You sound offended; are you?"

6. Mark replies, "No, I'm OK. Don't worry about me. I can take care of myself. I'm used to it. I just try to be nice to people and do people favors. If nobody ever thanks me for it or appreciates it, that's OK. I'll survive it."

7. Lillian says, "I'm hearing you say, 'Don't worry about me,' but yet you sound angry about not getting enough appreciation, and when I hear that, it tends to bother me. What's your reaction to that?"

8. Mark says, "I'm not angry! Just don't give it a second thought! Don't concern yourself with it! I'll be OK." (Self-pitying tone continues.)

9. Lillian says, "Well, I don't intend to punish myself and feel guilty over it, but it sure sounds like you haven't been getting enough appreciation to suit you. Maybe I can work on that in return for your working on the thing about touching. How does that sound?"
10. Mark says, "You don't need to work on anything. I told you, don't worry about it." (Mark starts to walk away.)
11. Lillian says, "See you later, Mark." (Her tone is cheerful, not guilty, self-accepting and accepting of Mark despite his sticking to the martyr stance.)

Note that in the above interchange, Mark is nonverbally asking Lillian to worry about him, to be concerned, to show appreciation, though verbally he is denying all of these messages. This sort of double message has been referred to by Bateson et al. as the "double bind." Lillian won't let herself get bound, though, because she picks up the nonverbal messages, comments on them, and therefore doesn't allow them to stay "underground." Yet she does so in an accepting way. She refuses to act guilty, and by not rewarding Mark for his martyr tactics, she encourages him eventually to give them up. (In the face of such facilitative messages, Mark might have stopped his verbal-nonverbal incongruity earlier, had not I, as author of this book, forced him to continue.)

Answers to Exercise 26

1. I Feel, I Want
2. Nonverbal Message of being offended
3. Asking for Feedback, Open-Ended Question
4. Verbal-Nonverbal Incongruity
5. Expressing Mixed Feelings, I Feel statement, Reflection of Feelings
6. Verbal-Nonverbal Incongruity
7. Reflection, I Feel, Asking for Feedback
8. Verbal-Nonverbal Incongruity

9. I Intend, Reflection, Bargaining, Asking for Feedback
10. Verbal-Nonverbal Incongruity, Communication Cutoff
11. Nonverbal "I'm OK, You're OK" message

8 Exercises: Speaking the Unspeakable

The dialogues in this chapter focus on messages that promote avoidance mechanisms which allow silence or vagueness to prevail when there is necessary communication to be done. Silent Resentment, Silent Need for Nurturance, and Assuming without Checking Out are silence producers, and Speaking about General Ways of Being and Indefinite Words and Phrases are vagueness and confusion producers. The antidotes to these are specific I Want and I Feel statements, Reflections, Citing Specific Behaviors, Direct Questions, and Asking for Specific Criticism.

Exercise 27
Romy and Julie Make Assumptions and Guesses

Go through this dialogue twice; the first time substitute a facilitative message for each of Julie's utterances; the second time do the same for Romy. Suggested responses are in parentheses. Possible answers are provided after the exercise.

1. Romy receives a traffic ticket on the way home. The policeman gives him a ticket for going 41 in a 35 mile an hour zone. Romy says nothing to the officer but just scowls as he gets the ticket. (Romy might try an I Want statement and Nonverbal Messages of I'm OK, You're OK, instead of Silent Resentment.)

2. Romy comes home in a bad mood because of this incident. Julie sees him in a bad mood and remembers that in the past Romy liked to hear *Rhapsody in Blue* when he was in a bad mood. So she puts on the record. (Instead of Assuming without Checking Out, Julie might make a Reflection and do some Mutual Topic Finding.)

3. Romy is sick of hearing *Rhapsody in Blue* because a house guest played it several times a day during a recent week while Julie was out of town. But Romy says nothing, thinking he will sacrifice for Julie. (Instead of this Silent Resentment, Romy might make an I Feel statement and an I Want statement about his preferences.)

4. Julie watches Romy's face and sees the anger that shows up. She remembers that Romy was angry at his boss last night and assumes that he is feeling bad because he is still angry with his boss. She puts a pillow in front of him and says, "Here, hit this pillow, and pretend it's Mr. Montague. Even yell and scream. It's something I learned in an encounter group: it'll make you feel better." (Instead of this Premature Advice and Assuming without Checking Out, Julie might make a Reflection and an Open-Ended Question.)

5. Romy thinks, "What a scatterbrain Julie is!" and he frowns. (Instead of using Silent Resentment, Romy might make a Reflection and a Self-Disclosure statement.)

6. Julie sees that Romy is frowning as he looks out the window in the direction of their son Cappy. She figures that Romy doesn't want to hit the pillow for fear that Cappy will walk in and be upset by the scene. So Julie says, "Send Cappy to the store down the street for a bottle of aspirin. That'll be a good idea." (Instead of this Assuming without Checking Out and Premature Advice, Julie might make a Reflection.)

7. Romy wanted to ask Cappy to help him do some work on his canoe, instead, but figures that Julie must have a

backache and decides he doesn't want to cross her if she's feeling bad. So he sends Cappy to the store, regretting that they can't work on the canoe now. (Instead of Silent Resentment, Romy might make a Reflection and an I Want statement.)

8. Romy, frustrated by all these events, looks at Julie with a very sour facial expression, picks up a magazine, then throws it down impatiently. (Romy might make some I Feel statements instead of Silent Resentment and Acting Out Anger.)

9. Julie, seeing him look at her disapprovingly, thinks that he doesn't like the outfit she is wearing. She says, "I'm going to go change clothes right now." (Instead of Assuming without Checking Out, Julie might make a Reflection.)

10. Romy figures that her clothes are too tight, and this may be why her back hurts. So he advises, "Why don't you put on your bathrobe?" (Instead of Assuming without Checking Out and Premature Advice, Romy might make a Reflection.)

11. Julie figures that this means that Romy is in the mood for a sexual encounter with her. She remembers that the doctor told them not to have intercourse until she gets over her infection. So she says, "But honey, don't you remember what the doctor said?" (Instead of Assuming without Checking Out and Using Indefinite Words and Phrases, Julie might make a Reflection.)

12. Romy remembers that the doctor told Julie she could wear whatever she wanted, because it wouldn't help or hurt her back. So he says, "OK, wear whatever you want to. I don't care." (Instead of Assuming what Julie meant, Romy might use a Direct Question.)

13. Julie hears this as a sexual rebuff. So she says, "Is that all it takes these days to persuade you? I think you should take some vitamin E." (Instead of giving Premature Advice and Using Indefinite Words and Phrases,

Julie might Reflect.)

14. Romy cannot make sense out of this last statement of Julie's to save his life. He assumes she is off her rocker and says, "I think you should go see a psychiatrist." (Instead of giving Premature Advice, Romy might ask Direct Questions.)

15. At this moment Cappy comes home with the aspirin. Julie says, "Cappy, take the aspirin to your father. I think he's irritated with his boss, and he's taking it out on me." (Instead of Expressing Dissatisfaction through a Third Party and Assuming without Checking Out, Julie might Reflect Feelings.)

By this time, Romy really does have a headache, so he takes it from Cappy with appreciation. As the story ends, Julie says, "Does that make you feel better?" Romy replies, "Yes, dear, thanks."

Possible Answers to Exercise 27
Translating for Julie (first time through)

2. "Romy, you look like you're in a bad mood. Would you like to talk about it, or hear some music, or anything?"

4. "Romy, you look angry. I'd be interested in hearing what's going on with you."

6. "Romy, I notice you're looking out the window where Cappy is. I have a fantasy that you're worrying that if you hit the pillow and Cappy comes in, it might upset him."

9. "Romy, I see you looking at me with what looks like a disapproving expression. I have a fantasy it's because you don't like my outfit. Is that right?"

11. "Romy, by asking me to put my bathrobe on, I am assuming that you are asking for us to make love. Is that right?"

13. "When you said that, Romy, I took it to mean that you didn't care whether we made love or not. You see, when

you asked me to put the bathrobe on, I thought that meant you wanted to make love. Was I right?"

15. "When you told me to see a psychiatrist just then, Romy, it seemed that you were upset with me. I have a fantasy that you're upset with your boss and taking it out on me. Is that right?"

Translating for Romy (second time through)

1. "Officer, I can see how you'd stop me. But if you have the discretionary power not to give me a ticket, I sure wish you wouldn't. I was going only a little over the limit."

3. "Julie, when I hear *Rhapsody in Blue* these days, it drives me up the wall because Mr. Mercutio played it every day while he was visiting the week before last. Unless you really want to hear it, in, which case I'll leave for a while, I'd like to turn it off."

5. "Julie, are you picking up on my anger and thinking that I'm mad at Mr. Montague right now? Actually I came home mad because I got a traffic ticket for going 41 in a 35 zone.

7. "Julie, I am assuming that you want the aspirin because you have a backache now. Is that right? If not, I'd like to get Cappy to help me work on the canoe instead."

8. "I'm feeling frustrated now. First, I got a ticket on the way home, which made me angry; then when you put on *Rhapsody in Blue* I felt tense because I've heard it so many times lately; then you wanted Cappy to get the aspirin, and I felt disappointed because I wanted him to help me work on the canoe now."

10. "Julie, I have a fantasy that you're wanting to change clothes because your back hurts. Is that right?"

12. "Which doctor, at what time? I don't think I know what you're talking about."

14. "I don't understand, Julie. Persuade me of what? And what does vitamin E have to do with changing your clothes?

Exercise 28
Cleo and Jules Do Some Vague
and Indefinite and Unenjoyable Talking

Each statement below is an example of Speaking about General Ways of Being or Indefinite Words and Phrases. Go through the dialogue twice, first translating for Cleo, then for Jules. Make each statement cite Specific Behaviors, making up any specific behaviors that you want that might apply in the context. Possible answers are given after the exercise.

1. Cleo and Jules are talking about their son Tony. Jules says, "I've been worried about Tony lately. He seems so sensitive."

2. Cleo replies, "Why should you worry about that? His being sensitive is just what I like about him the most."

3. Jules replies, "You really are strange."

4. Jules continues, "It doesn't surprise me that you would encourage him to be that way since you are such a fragile person yourself."

5. Cleo replies, "Well at least I'm not callous like you are."

6. Cleo continues, "And you're not only callous. You're cold."

7. Jules replies, "Your trouble is that you want me to be an angel. But I'm not an angel. I'm just a person. You can't seem to understand that."

8. Cleo replies, "No, you're not an angel, but what's more, you really are cruel at times."

9. Jules replies, "Somebody ought to take out your tongue and put in a new one, do you know that?"

10. Cleo says, "Another thing about you is that when you and Tony are around, you think only about yourself."

11. Jules replies, "Yeah? Well when it comes to doing anything vigorous, you are totally passive. You're just like a bag of potatoes."

12. At this moment Tony comes in from playing and tracks some dirt on the living room rug. Cleo says, "Tony, oh,

look. You're a bad boy."

13. Jules says, "Why do you always have to be so picky, Cleo?"
14. Cleo replies, "You sure don't know anything about raising kids, Jules."
15. Cleo then says to Tony, "Tony, you're being a slob. Don't be that way."
16. Tony runs to Jules, looks at Cleo, and says, "You're mean."
17. Cleo replies to Tony, "Oh, you're spoiled rotten! Your father has spoiled you rotten!"
18. Jules storms out the front door, saying, "The both of you are too much to take!"

Possible Answers to Exercise 28
Translating for Cleo (first time through)

2. Instead of this, Cleo could say, "I like the fact that Tony can pick up on what somebody is thinking or feeling and comment to them about it in a sympathetic tone of voice, like, for example, the way he was talking with Aunt Mabel the other night."
5. Instead of this, Cleo could say, "When I'm upset, I wish you would sit down and talk with me and listen. Instead, you often seem to have an uncaring or angry look on your face, which makes me feel rejected."
6. Instead of this, Cleo could say, "And at times like that I would like you to touch me more. Last night, when I was upset over what happened at work, is an example."
8. Instead of this, Cleo could say, "Another thing I'd like you not to do is to yell at me and tell me to buckle down and take it when I'm feeling upset. I'd like you to say some gentle things to me."
10. Instead of this, Cleo could say, "One thing I've been meaning to ask you is that when you and Tony and I are together, could you please support me when I try to en-

force a rule with Tony, instead of taking Tony's side?"

12. Instead of this, Cleo could say, "Tony, when it's raining I'd like you to take off your shoes at the door and leave them on the doormat so that you won't get the rug dirty and I won't have such a hard time cleaning it up, OK?"

14. Instead of this, Cleo could say, "Jules, I wish that you would be more active in telling Tony about things we don't like him to do, such as tracking mud on the rug. That way I wouldn't have to do it so much myself. I feel like I'm doing it much more than you are."

15. Instead of this, Cleo could say, "Tony, I'd like it if you would clean the mud off the rug before it dries."

17. Instead of this, Cleo could say, "When you say I'm mean, I sure don't like hearing that, although maybe there's some truth in it."

Translating for Jules (second time through)

1. Instead of this, Jules could say, "I've been worried by the fact that when someone criticizes Tony, he seems to pout and look downcast for quite some time afterward."

3. Instead of this, Jules could say, "When you said just then that you liked his being sensitive, it surprised me because I don't think of sensitive as a good way to be."

4. Instead of this, Jules could say, "The behaviors I'm seeing in Tony remind me of some in you. When I criticize you and when you pout and won't talk afterwards, that makes me feel guilty and upset."

7. Instead of this, Jules could say, "When you call me callous and cold, that hurts me."

9. Instead of this, Jules could say, "When you call me cruel, that really hurts and makes me angry, too."

11. Instead of this, Jules could say, "I think it would help things if you could go hiking or camping with Tony and

me, and maybe learn to tolerate it more when Tony's and my clothes aren't neat and clean."

13. Instead of this, Jules could say, "Cleo, I'd like you to point out more things that you like about what Tony's done and to pick on him less for things that you don't like. And I think I'd like the same for myself. What do you think about that?"

18. Instead of this, Jules could say, "The way we've been calling each other names for the last few minutes is unpleasant for me."

Exercise 29
Ralph and Betty Don't Say What They Want
and Therefore Don't Get It

In the following scenario, degrees of wants and feelings are expressed rather vaguely. Translate them into more precisely quantified wants or feelings, using either words like "not at all," "slightly," "moderately," and "extremely"; or use a numerical scale, such as 0 to 10. If you can't tell from the conversation how much the person wants a certain thing or feels a certain thing, make up any quantity you wish. Translate first for Betty, then for Ralph.

Situation: Betty and Ralph are in the car, on their way to a furniture store to look at a couch. As they are traveling, Ralph says, "Oh, by the way, Betty, the MacGillicutties have invited us over for an open house they are having on Wednesday night. Would you like to go?"

1. Ralph continues, "I don't much care myself." (Actually Ralph would very slightly rather stay at home, but he's not accustomed to making fine distinctions because he doesn't want to influence Betty. Translate this into a Quantification.)

2. Betty replies, "What ever you want is fine with me." (Actually Betty would slightly rather stay at home, too.

147

Translate into a Quantification that reflects this.)

Ralph says, "The party might be fun . . . ," trying to feel out what Betty really wants. Betty, thinking that this means that Ralph wants to go, says, "Well, it would be fine with me if we go." Ralph replies, "Well, OK, let's go then." Betty agrees. At that moment they arrive at the furniture store and look at several couches. At the end of their deliberations, they are choosing among three couches: a vinyl one, a yellow fabric-covered one, and a green fabric-covered one. Ralph says, "What do you think?"

3. Betty replies, "That yellow one is pretty nice, but then again that green one is awful pretty, too. The vinyl would be nice, too, I guess, if you like it. That seems to be the sort of couch you'd like, you know?" (Translate this into any Quantification that clearly expresses degrees of preference among the three couches.)

4. Ralph replies, "Well, I could see getting any one of the three; whichever one you want is fine. Is that yellow one your first choice?" (Ralph guesses this from the fact that Betty mentioned the yellow one first. Translate this statement of Ralph's into any Quantification that clearly expresses degrees of preference among the three couches.)

Betty says, "I could see getting the yellow one, could you?" (Actually she slightly prefers the green one.)

Ralph replies, "Yes, let's go ahead and get that one then, OK?" And they get it. Actually Ralph greatly preferred the green one to the yellow one, but he wanted to get what Betty wanted, so he "sacrificed."

As they drive home, they pass the Burger King. As they approach, Ralph says, "Do you want to stop and get a hamburger?"

5. Betty says, "At the Burger King? I don't know. Do you really want to?" (Actually Betty would really like to stop and get a hamburger somewhere, but she hesitates

because she would to a moderate degree prefer McDonald's to the Burger King. Translate her statement into one that clearly quantifies these wants.)

6. Ralph says, "I don't guess so—I can last." (Actually Ralph would like to stop at a hamburger joint, and it doesn't make any difference to him whether it's at Burger King or McDonald's. But because he senses the hesitancy in Betty's voice, he drives on. Translate his statement into one that clearly quantifies his wants.)

    There have now been three times when Ralph has given in to decisions differently from the way he would have wanted to. He looks a little irritated from this. Betty picks this up and says, "Ralph, are you feeling irritated? Do you wish we'd gotten the green couch?"

7. Ralph says, "Yeah, I am feeling irritated over that." (Actually Ralph doesn't really care too much about the couches. His main irritation is over not stopping to eat. And he doesn't feel very great irritation over either issue. Make a statement that quantifies his feelings and wants.)

    Betty says, "Well, let's go back then and get the green one instead. I liked that one better myself."

8. Ralph replies, "No, let's not do that." (Actually the reason he doesn't want to do that is that it is quite a distance back to the furniture store, and he would prefer having the extra time to relax, much more than he cares about the difference between the yellow and green couch. Make a statement for him that will quantify his preferences.)

    Betty, not wishing to make Ralph irritated, begs him to go back to the store, and he finally turns around and starts back. After doing this he looks even more irritated and angry. Now Betty doesn't know why he is angry so she says, "What's making you angry now?"

9. Ralph replies, "Oh, I don't know. This whole thing just drives me up the wall." (Actually Ralph is most upset

over the driving time this is taking. He is next most upset over not stopping to get something to eat, and next most upset over how Betty kept begging him to turn back when he didn't want to. (Make a statement that quantifies the importance of these feelings for the sake of Betty's information.)

Betty hears this as a general comment on their relationship and gets scared by it. She asks, "Ralph, are you thinking that our marriage isn't working out?"

10. Ralph replies, "No, our marriage is fine. We don't have any problems. Don't go asking stupid questions like this." (Actually Ralph has no doubt that he wants to stay with Betty, but he is rather upset with this evening's events. Make a statement that will quantify his desire to stay with her and the feeling of being upset so that Betty can separate the two in her own mind.)

Betty takes what Ralph just said as being sarcastic and gets very frightened that Ralph is thinking of leaving her. She wants very much to stay with him.

11. Betty says, "Are you trying to get me to leave you? Are you trying to get rid of me?" (By this time Betty is almost in tears. Make a statement that quantifies both her desire to stay with Ralph and her fear that he will leave her and that verbalizes her Silent Wish for Nurturance.)

Ralph yells, "If you want a divorce, just ask for it. That's all you have to do if you don't love me!" Betty bursts into tears and sobs uncontrollably. Ralph pulls over to the side of the road, apologizes profusely, and Betty apologizes profusely also. Betty says, "Ralph, let's go home. My head's killing me." And they do.

Possible Answers to Exercise 29
Translating for Betty (first time through)

2. "I'd enjoy going to the open house, but I'd slightly prefer staying home. I'd prefer it by only 1 or 2 on a

scale of 10, so if you prefer to go by more than that, I'd be more than willing to go."

3. "I like the green couch about 9 on a scale of 10, the yellow one about 8, and the vinyl around 5."

5. "I'd really like to stop and get a hamburger, but between the Burger King and the McDonald's around the corner, I'd moderately prefer the McDonald's. What are your preferences?"

Or: "If not stopping at all is 2 on a scale of 10, stopping at the Burger King is 7, but stopping at McDonald's would be 10."

11. "Ralph, I want to stay with you extremely much, and I'm very, very frightened at the idea that you would leave me. I would like some reassurance now."

Translating for Ralph (second time through)

1. "I would like to go to the party about 7 on a 0 to 10 scale, whereas I would also like staying home and watching TV with you about 8."

4. "I like the green one 10 on a scale of 10, and the yellow one and the vinyl are each about 6 for me."

6. "Burger King and McDonald's are about equal to me, but I'd prefer stopping at one of them to going straight home by about 8 on a scale of 10."

7. "Betty, if 10 is the most irritated I've ever felt, and 0 is totally nonirritated, then not getting the green couch irritates me one unit, and not stopping to eat irritates me three units."

8. "Betty, I'd prefer the green couch by about 3 on a scale of 10, but I'd prefer to go on home and not worry about it any more by about 9. So I want to go on home."

Or: "Betty, I only slightly prefer the green couch, but I extremely prefer to go home and not spend any more time driving."

9. "Betty, there are a few things making me upset. Spend-

ing all this time driving is upsetting me about 6 on a scale of 10. Not getting something to eat is upsetting me 4; and the way you kept telling me to turn around also irritated me some, maybe 3."

10. "Betty, I want to stay with you 10 on a scale of 10, but I'm upset over this particular evening about 7 on a scale of 10."

Or: "Betty, there's no doubt at all in my mind that I want us to stay together. However, this evening has been fairly frustrating to me."

Exercise 30
Making Specific Behaviors from
General Ways of Being (for two people to practice)

The purpose of this exercise is to train you to think in terms of Specific Behaviors and to translate from general words to specific ones.

The first person calls out a general adjective, such as warm, considerate, friendly, generous, passive, domineering, hostile, obnoxious, etc. The second person then visualizes a specific behavior that could be an example of that general adjective.

If the behavior is one that has actually occurred, the second person says, "I liked it when you did x," or "I didn't like it when you did x." If the behavior has not occurred, but it is imaginary, the second person may say, "I would like it if you did x" or "I wouldn't like it if you did y."

Examples:

First person: "Warm."

Second person: "I liked it when you rubbed my back yesterday morning as we were waking up."

First person: "Hostile."

Second person: "I would like it if when a salesman came by and wouldn't leave, you would raise your voice at him and order him out."

First person: "Hostile."

Second person: "I wouldn't like it if one day you walked out of the room when we were talking and slammed the door."

The point of the exercise is not to pick behaviors that are particularly good examples of the adjectives, but to get practice in translating from the vague language of the adjectives to more specific language of concrete images.

9 Encouraging the Other Person to Talk and Explore

Sometimes, when people are solving problems, they don't need to define the problem and start listing options quickly. Sometimes one or both of them need time to think about the problem, to talk about it in a permissive climate, and to think out loud. Self-disclosure by one or both people sometimes clarifies and redefines the issue to the point where the problem nearly takes care of itself.

Exercise 31
Using Reflections Instead of Premature Advice

Premature Advice is one message that tends to curtail self-disclosure by the other, whereas accurate and accepting Reflections tend to encourage self-disclosure. In the following dialogue substitute a Reflection for each of Jean's Premature Advice responses. Answers are provided after the exercise.

Jean gives Premature Advice to Harry. Each of the numbered responses of Jean is an example of Premature Advice. Translate each into a Reflection.

Situation: Harry says in a tired, disgusted tone of voice, "This boss of mine is really something. I've never seen such a person."
1. Jean replies, "Well, if you don't like him, do something about it! Tell him off! Stick up for yourself!" (Substi-

tute a Reflection.)

Harry replies, "It's just that he expects you to give body and soul to the company, just like he does. If he likes his two heart attacks, that's fine, but he seems to want all us employees to drive ourselves to heart attacks too!"

2. Jean replies, "Don't be silly. You're in good health. Your doctor told you so. Get another checkup if you're worried. Otherwise forget it." (Substitute a Reflection.)

   Harry replies, "Can you imagine what it would be like to have had a heart attack and now to know that just by shoveling snow too hard you could keel over and breathe your last?"

3. Jean replies, "You worry needlessly! Don't cross your bridges until you come to them." (Substitute a Reflection.)

   Harry replies, "I don't know. I just can't help wondering about this whole lifestyle."

4. Jean replies, "What is there to wonder about? It's too late to change it now. You can't start all over, so you might as well just learn to live with it." (Substitute a Reflection.)

   Harry replies, "It just doesn't seem to be worth the sacrifice I'm making now. I feel like I'm killing myself working."

5. Jean replies, "You're killing yourself? That means you're taking work too seriously. Do what I do: think some happy thoughts while you're working. It'll cheer you up." (Substitute a Reflection.)

   Harry replies, "I don't know about that, but I'm thinking of insisting on regular hours and not staying overtime and not bringing work home."

6. Jean replies, "And while you're at it, you ought to just give that boss a piece of your mind. Yell and scream at him some. It'll make you feel better to discharge some emotion." (Substitute a Reflection.)

Note: This conversation is somewhat unrealistic, since Harry was able to move toward a solution to the problem despite the roadblocks put in the way by Jean's Premature Advice. In reality he probably would have felt obligated to respond in some way to the solutions she proposed. If she had used Reflections rather than Premature Advice, his job would have been easier.

Possible Answers to Exercise 31

1. "Sounds like he kinda gets to you, huh?"
2. "It's pretty scary to think of wrecking yourself from overwork the way he does, isn't it?"
3. "Boy, that is a worrisome idea. The whole image of you getting a heart attack is really scary."
4. "You're wondering if it's worth the sacrifice you're making now?"
5. "Are you saying you want to make some changes in the way things are?"
6. "It sounds like the idea really pleases you!"

Exercise 32   A Role-Playing or Real-Life Exercise
Interviewing the Other

In this exercise, one person is the interviewer, and the other is the interviewee. The interviewer is to find out all that he can about the other and is to avoid Premature Advice, Defending Oneself, You Did Something Bad, and all other messages that would sidetrack the interviewee from talking about himself and his thoughts and feelings. The interviewer is to make heavy use of Reflections. The interviewee is to Self-Disclose as much as he feels comfortable doing. After a time, the two people switch roles, and the second person interviews the first.

This exercise is particularly helpful for people who feel that "We've spent time together, but we don't really know each other." (This applies to some people who have been together for years, also. It's better late than never!)

10 Some More Role-Playing and Real-Life Exercises

1. Reflecting after Each Communication

One person makes a statement. The second person responds by Reflecting what the other said or implied, and the first person responds either "yes," "no" or "partly." The second person keeps trying until she gets a yes. Then she makes any statement, and the first person Reflects; thus they alternate. Another way to do this exercise is to have the second person make Reflections until she gets not one but three "yeses." This way of doing it illustrates that any statement carries more than one message.

2. I Want and I Feel with Reflection in Response

The first person makes an I Want or I Feel statement; the second responds with a Reflection. The first person answers "yes," "no" or "partly." When a yes is obtained, they switch.

3. Responding to Criticism

The first person makes a criticism of any sort, adaptive or maladaptive, true or false. The second responds as quickly as possible with as many of the following as possible: Agreeing with Part of Criticism, Asking for More Specific Criticism, Reflection, I Feel, and I Want or Bargaining. Then they switch.

After about 15 minutes, or at a good stopping point, switch again.

4. Exercise in Nonverbal Messages of "I'm OK, You're OK"

The first person makes up a sentence, and the second person then says that sentence in each of the following three ways:

A. With lack of self-confidence (I'm not OK; placating; scared; submissive)

B. With lack of acceptance of the other (You're not OK; blaming; hostile)

C. With self-confidence and acceptance of the other (I'm OK, You're OK; firm; self-assured)

Try sentences like these:

"I burned the rolls."

"Would you mind taking out the garbage for me?"

"Yes, it looks like I've made a mistake."

"How about letting me finish talking."

"Let's figure out what we did wrong."

"Why did you do it that way?"

"What's going on?"

"It's raining outside."

You will find that almost any sentence can be said realistically in each of these three ways.

5. Recipe for a Nonproductive Fight

Each person chooses from the list of obstructive messages and cannot use any others. Special emphasis is given to You Are Bad and You Did Bad, Defending Oneself, Put-Down Questions, Sarcasm, and Threats.

As you pick from the list, feel which obstructive messages are most natural for you to use and notice whether you use the same ones in "real life." Notice what types of messages from the other person most strongly spur your obstructive responses.

When doing this exercise in role playing, pick things to say about the other that aren't true.

6. Responding Facilitatively to Obstructive Messages

In the real world, people don't always use facilitative messages. In fact it's sometimes more the exception than the rule. Therefore, a very important ability to cultivate is that of responding with facilitative messages even when the other person is using obstructive ones.

In this exercise, the first person is to use as obstructive messages as possible, and the second person is to respond with facilitative messages. Then turn the tables: the second person gets to practice responding to the obstructive messages. Use situations given in this book, or any other situations.

Some examples of dialogues of this sort are given in exercises 19 and 25.

7. Practice in Facilitative Messages

Two people have a conversation, one dealing with some chosen conflict situation or an open-ended one. The constraint is that each must only use messages on the facilitative list. Eliminate Speaking about External Events and Direct Questions to make this exercise more challenging.

8. Special Exercises to Break Particularly Ingrained Habits

If you are in the habit of using a particular sort of obstructive message, make up exercises in which first you exaggerate the message and use it to ridiculous excess in order to sensitize yourself to its use.

Then pick suitable alternatives to the obstructive message from the list of facilitative messages and practice using them over and over again in place of the obstructive one. (Examples: Asking for Feedback vs. Overlong Statements; I Want or I Feel in place of You Are Bad; Reflections vs. Premature Advice; Bargaining vs. Commanding; Citing Specific Behaviors vs. Speaking about General Ways of Being; Agreeing with Criticism vs. Defending Oneself.)

11 A Catalogue of Problems to Practice Solving

Use these exercises to practice interpersonal problem solving. Add conflicts from your own experience to the list.

1. Bob and Ted are roommates. Bob owns a typewriter that he hardly ever uses. It is in need of some repairs before it will be usable. Ted is going to need to do some typing and would like to use Bob's typewriter after it is repaired. However, Ted doesn't want to pay the full cost of the repair just to borrow the typewriter, and Bob doesn't want to spend much money on repairing something he hardly ever uses.

2. René and Frank are neighbors. Frank has a dog, Henrietta, that he allows to run loose. Everyone in the neighborhood except René loves Henrietta. It seems that René has a tropical flower garden, which is one of Henrietta's favorite places to roll in the dirt and bury bones, digging up and crushing flowers in the process.

3. LeRoy lives in an apartment directly over that of Chen. LeRoy practices Kung Fu every evening and in doing so jumps around a lot, making a racket that comes through the floor to disturb Chen. Every morning Chen listens to soul music on his stereo, played very loudly, and LeRoy, who likes only classical music, is disturbed.

4. Alex and Ruth are married. Ruth's parents live nearby, and she likes to go and see them at least once a week

and to take Alex along. Ruth's parents have various customs that Alex doesn't like, and it is unpleasant for him to visit as often as Ruth likes to visit.

5. Jim and Cathy have a joint checking account, and each of them has a checkbook. It is hard for them to keep up with how much the other has spent, and sometimes when both of them spend a lot of money at the same time, they overdraw their checking account.

6. On two different occasions Cathy has made pies to give away to friends. When the friends came over to pick up the pie, however, she has been embarrassed to find that Jim has eaten at least half of the pie, not knowing that it was to be given away.

7. Mildred likes to have her daughter Mabel visit her, but every time Mabel gets ready to leave, Mildred begs her not to leave so soon. She accuses Mabel of not loving her, saying, "Or else why would you want to leave so soon?" Sometimes Mabel stays a little longer in response to this behavior. Mabel likes visiting, but she doesn't like having these scenes at the end of each visit.

Some Work Situations

8. Fred is Sam's boss. Fred assigns Sam to do a project which Sam considers a waste of time. Fred also believes that the project is not useful, but he would rather go ahead and have Sam do it than contend with *his* boss, Mr. Bilgewater, who believes that the project is worthwhile.

9. Gene is accustomed to wearing a turtleneck and sandals, and this attire is frowned upon by his boss, Elnora, who feels that a suit would be more appropriate.

10. John and Betty work in different departments. Neither is obligated to the other. John has some specialized work that he needs done, which can only be done by Betty. Yet Betty has nothing to gain from doing the work. In fact, since the work would take time away

from the tasks that her boss has given her, she will lose time by doing the work for John.

11. The "chain of command" is that Alice supervises Lance, who in turn supervises Jean. On several occasions Jean has consulted directly with Alice without notifying Lance. Then Lance has been embarrassed in conversation with Alice because he was not aware of arrangements that Jean has made with Alice. Jean has found Lance sometimes difficult to get in touch with to check things out.

12. Frank and Sam share the same secretary. Frank tends to procrastinate and often gives the secretary "rush jobs." Furthermore, he is more inclined to designate something as a rush job than Sam is. Because of this, Sam notices that the secretary tends to put off his work. Sam has spoken to the secretary about this, with no results.

13. Joan has an employee that she wishes to fire. This employee makes frequent costly mistakes and also frequently causes quarrels among his co-workers. Joan's supervisor, Mark, does not want Joan to fire this employee because then Mark would have to put up with many hassles from the Employee Relations Department, plus a possible suit by the employee.

14. Ted and Mike have worked together on a research project and have written a paper reporting their results. They are ready to submit the paper to a journal. They have both worked about equally in conceiving and designing the project and working on it. When they submit the paper, one will be the first author and the other will be the second author. Each would prefer to be first.

15. Frances is a medical student who is assigned to Sandra, who is a doctor. When Sandra treats patients, Frances, wishing to be educated, very frequently asks Sandra questions about the patients and about other medical topics. Sandra finds it quite draining to be answering these questions so frequently when she is trying to do

other things, such as read the patients' charts, write consultation notes, find materials, and so forth.

16. Marsha likes to talk about her personal life with Jane. Jane likes these talks, but lately they have been hindering Jane in her work.

17. Marcus, who is Peter's boss, watches very closely over what Peter does. He supervises every step and wants very frequent reports. Peter feels uncomfortable at being under such close surveillance.

18. Ralph is Michael's boss. Michael is in the habit of griping to other employees about some of Ralph's policies, and Ralph is worried about the morale of these other employees. Michael believes that his freedom to speak his mind is very important.

19. About a month ago, the following incident occurred: Raul, the supervisor, received word from some employees that Simon, a new employee, had stolen some items from the store. Raul checked on what these items were and called Simon in to confront him with this accusation. Simon vigorously denied stealing and furnished proof that the items were not stolen but bought from another store. Raul apologized, and the incident was over.

However, from then on, Simon has looked at Raul and some of his fellow employees with bitter and resentful facial expressions and has spoken with a sullen tone of voice.

Some Silly Situations

The principles of communication used in negotiating these silly situations are the same as those used with other situations. Many times I think it's helpful to have some comic relief when practicing problem solving. I have heard some very creative interchanges when people have used these situations for practicing communication.

20. You and I are next door neighbors. You are building a

statue in your back yard. I think that this statue is not something I want to look at and want you to take it down. You think that just because the statue is of an elephant dancing in undershorts is no reason for it to come down, especially when it's on your own property.

21. You and I are best friends. I always forget to give you a Columbus Day card or to wish you a happy Columbus Day, which offends you because you are a direct descendent of Christopher Columbus. I have just forgotten again.

22. You and I are roommates. You love sauerkraut better than any other food. However, I have a very delicate cat who is so allergic to sauerkraut that even the fumes from cooking cause the poor cat to sniffle, sneeze, itch, and break out.

23. You and I live together. You have some plants that you are very fond of. However, the plants have not been doing well because of their getting too much water, and we have lately discovered that I have been sleepwalking in the middle of the night and watering the plants during my walks.

24. You are an ardent member of the Underwriters United to Overthrow the Underworld (UUOU). You talk all the time about the organization's activities and how the ideas of the organization will probably be the main salvation of the world. I don't want to participate myself and get tired of hearing about the whole thing.

25. You and I are married. I owe a tremendous debt of gratitude to my Uncle George, who saved me from certain disaster by pushing me out of the way of a French horn that had fallen out of a twentieth story window onto the sidewalk beside us. He is visiting us now, and he snores so loudly that he keeps you awake at night.

26. You and I are co-workers. I am blessed with the ability to do imitations and impressions and can do excellent impressions of Woody Allen, Jimmy Carter, Mae West,

and assorted barnyard animals including a perfect imitation of a turkey gobble. You have taken advantage of this ability by bringing around certain selected clients to hear my imitations. You feel that the entire success of our "frozen turkey" line of air conditioners is due to the fact that clients just can't resist after having heard my gobble. However, I am tired of being used in this way.

27. I am your boss. I think that your moonlighting job as a goldfish-swallower at a local night club brings bad publicity to our business, which distributes pet store products. You think that what you do in your off-hours is your own business.

28. You and I are co-workers. My hobby is playing melodies using the touch-tone telephone in the office. I am quite accomplished at this and can play Beethoven's *Moonlight Sonata* and many other good songs. You find that this ties up the line too much for you.

Some Situations between Spouses

29. Jenny drives too slowly to suit her husband Ted; Ted would like her to be more aggressive. When she drives them somewhere, Ted gives frequent suggestions to Jenny; these irritate her.

30. Jack thinks that his wife Jean wears too much make-up; Jean considers that her make-up is not part of Jack's business.

31. Sheila likes to work out with weights at home. When her husband Tom sees her, Tom is in the habit of saying, "Come on! One more! Push! Don't stop!" Sheila, on the other hand, would like to be thinking about other things while lifting and considers Tom's exhortations to be irritating distractions.

32. Rob is in the habit of thinking for a second or two in silence before replying to what someone has said. His

wife Lisa, on the other hand, is in the habit of responding instantly as soon as the other person finishes talking. When they have friends visit, therefore, Lisa tends to do a lot of talking and to feel that Rob is acting withdrawn; Rob feels that Lisa is dominating the floor too much.

33. Kevin believes that unions exploit workers and create inflation and inefficiency, whereas his wife Nancy believes that unions are all that save workers from the ruthlessness of corporations. Whenever the topic comes up, they argue so heatedly that they get very angry at each other.

34. In Carmen's family, people often raised their voices at one another when they wanted something of the other person. In her husband Ingmar's family, people never raised their voices under any circumstances except when they felt nearly murderous rage. Ingmar reacts very negatively when Carmen raises her voice at him.

35. Tom loves to talk about sports; his wife Jennifer is not interested in sports at all and considers them a waste of time. When Tom starts to talk about sports, Jennifer gets bored and irritated quickly.

36. Jake likes to spend a lot of time watching television. Sandy thinks that the television contains so many bad models for their children that she would prefer that they not even own one.

37. Jim has a much higher preference for order and neatness than does his wife Susan. Jim therefore is irritated by the fact that Susan leaves things scattered around.

38. Tim will feel secure financially only if he and his wife can build up their savings very substantially. He therefore wants to consume very little for the present. His wife Gina believes more in living for the moment without having to build up savings so quickly. On many expenditures, then, they disagree.

Sources for the Messages

I would like to acknowledge the sources for the concepts of various messages described in this book. The terms Open-Ended Question and Direct Question were explained in *Medical Interviewing: A Programmed Manual*, by Froelich and Bishop (10). Reflections have been advocated by various people and have come from many sources. The concepts may have been begun by Carl Rogers (18, 19), who uses these techniques very skillfully in therapy. These have also been advocated by Thomas Gordon in *Parent Effectiveness Training* (11) under the name of Active Listening. I Feel statements and Listing Options and Choosing among Them also have been discussed by Gordon under the names of I-messages and No-lose Conflict-Solving Method. I-messages have also been written about by Salter (20), whom Wolpe (30) calls "the pioneer of assertive techniques." The idea for I Want statements came from Virginia Satir's *Conjoint Family Therapy* (21), specifically Chapter 9, entitled "Communication: A Verbal and Nonverbal Process of Making Requests of the Receiver." The idea for Bargaining came from the school of behaviorally oriented marital therapists, e.g., Richard Stuart (24), Robert Weiss (29), David Knox (14), and Nathan Azrin et al. (1), who in turn derived some of their ideas from the social exchange theories of Thibaut and Kelley (28). The idea of Citing Specific Behaviors as opposed to Speaking about General Ways of Being also came from this school. This concept was discussed by Stuart (24) using the terms "molar" vs. "molecular" descriptions of behavior. The idea of Quantification of Wants and Feelings is also a logical outgrowth of "social exchange" notions. Agreeing with Part of a Criticism or Argument, called fogging, and Asking for More Specific Criticism, called negative inquiry, appeared and were defined in *When I Say No I Feel Guilty* by Manuel J. Smith (23). Self-disclosure was discussed in this book as well as in numerous other sources, e.g., *The Transparent Self* by Sidney Jourard (13). The idea of Nonverbal Messages of "I'm OK, You're OK" is borrowed from the transactional analysts, of whom Eric Berne (4) was the seminal thinker. The idea of nonverbal communication has been widely propagated in recent years; *Body Language* (8) has been one of my sources, as have been the writings of Virginia Satir (21). The study of nonverbal communication has been reviewed by Swensen (27). The idea of Verbal-Nonverbal Incongruity was taken from the "double bind" hypothesis introduced by Bateson, Jackson, Haley, and Weakland (3). Commanding, Threatening, and Premature Advice were discussed by Gordon (11) in *P.E.T.*; You Are Bad and You Did Bad statements are derivatives of the "you messages" discussed in his book. You Should statements and the notion of "should" in general have been widely inveighed against; the writings of Albert Ellis (7) and Fritz Perls (17) provide examples. Overgeneralizing was discussed in *Conjoint Family Therapy* (21). The perils of Silent Resentment have been discussed at least since the beginning of assertiveness training; Joseph Wolpe (30) and Andrew Salter (20) deserve credit in this area. The idea for Attacking with a New Issue came from *The Intimate Enemy*, by Bach and Wyden (2). The notion of Silent Need for Nurturance has its intellectual origin in a discussion of "dependence fear" by F. R. Hine (12), who incorporates the notions of the Leary interpersonal circle (15); Silent Need for

Nurturance is to "dependence fear" as Silent Resentment is to "aggression fear." The I Intend statement is suggested by the "independence" or "dominance" portion of the Leary interpersonal circle, as well as by the writings of Murray Bowen (5) on the individuation of married individuals. The extension of the notion of desensitization to include fears of ways of relating and feeling, which underlies the strategy of gradual practice in more and more emotion-charged situations for role playing, was suggested by the writings of Feather and Rhoads (9), as well as by the pioneering work of Wolpe (30). The use of the interpersonal circle, the notion of social exchange, and the idea of behavior (such as Acting Out Anger or Need for Nurturance) as being motivated by the expectation of interpersonal outcomes are all ideas coming via *Interaction Concepts of Personality* by Robert C. Carson (6). The concept of shaping has been discussed widely, e.g., by Skinner (22). The use of self-rewarding (as opposed to self-punishing) internal sentences was advocated by Ellis (7); further work on this area was reviewed by Mahoney (16). The use of rehearsal in fantasy as a method of practice for athletes has been described by Richard M. Suinn (25, 26).

1. Azrin, N. H., Naster, B. J., and Jones, R. Reciprocity counseling: A rapid learning-based procedure for marital counseling. *Behaviour Research and Therapy,* 1973, *11,* 365-82.

2. Bach, G. R., and Wyden, P. *The intimate enemy: How to fight fair in love and marriage.* New York: William Morrow & Co., Inc., 1968.

3. Bateson, G., Jackson, D. D., Haley, J., and Weakland, J. Toward a theory of schizophrenia. *Behavioral Science,* 1956, *1,* 251-64.

4. Berne, E. *Principles of group treatment.* New York: Oxford University Press, 1966.

5. Bowen, M. The use of family theory in clinical practice. *Comprehensive Psychiatry,* 1966, *7,* 345-74.

6. Carson, R. C. *Interaction concepts of personality*. Chicago: Aldine, 1969.

7. Ellis, A., and Harper, R. *A guide to rational living*. Englewood Cliffs, NJ: Prentice-Hall, 1961.

8. Fast, J. *Body language*. New York: M. Evans and Co., 1970.

9. Feather, B. W., and Rhoads, J. M. Psychodynamic behavior therapy. *Archives of General Psychiatry*, 1972, *26*, 496-517.

10. Froelich, R. E., and Bishop, F. M. *Medical interviewing: A programmed manual*. St. Louis: C. V. Mosby, 1972.

11. Gordon, T. *P.E.T. Parent effectiveness training: The tested new way to raise responsible children*. New York: Wyden, 1970.

12. Hine, F. R. *Introduction to psychodynamics: A conflict adaptational approach*. Durham, NC: Duke University Press, 1971.

13. Jourard, S. M. *The transparent self*. Princeton, NJ: Van Nostrand, 1964.

14. Knox, D. *Dr. Knox's marital exercise book*. New York: David McKay, 1975.

15. Leary, T. *Interpersonal diagnosis of personality—A functional theory and methodology for personality evaluation*. New York: Ronald Press, 1957.

16. Mahoney, M. J. The cognitive therapies: Cognitive restructuring and self-instruction. Chapter 11 in Mahoney, M. J., *Cognition and behavior modification*. Cambridge, MA: Ballinger Publishing Co., 1974.

17. Perls, F. S. *Gestalt therapy verbatim*. Moab, UT: Real People Press, 1969.

18. Rogers, C. R. *Counseling and psychotherapy*. Boston: Houghton Mifflin, 1942.

19. Rogers, C. R. *On becoming a person*. Boston: Houghton Mifflin, 1961.

20. Salter, A. *Conditioned reflex therapy*. New York: Creative Age, 1949.

21. Satir, V. S. *Conjoint family therapy*. Palo Alto: Science and Behavior Books, Inc., 1967.

22. Skinner, B. F. *Science and human behavior*. New York: Free Press, 1953.

23. Smith, M. J. *When I say no, I feel guilty*. New York: Dial Press, 1975.

24. Stuart, R. B. Operant-interpersonal treatment for marital discord. *Journal of Consulting and Clinical Psychology*, 1969, *33*, 675-82.

25. Suinn, R. M. Behavior rehearsal training for ski racers. *Behavior Therapy*, 1972, *3*, 519-20.

26. Suinn, R. M. Body thinking: Psychology for Olympic champs. *Psychology Today*, July 1976, 38-43.

27. Swensen, C. H. Proxemics, kinesics, and paralanguage. Chapter 4 in *Introduction to interpersonal relations*. Glenview, IL: Scott, Foresman and Co., 1973.

28. Thibaut, J. W., and Kelley, H. H. *The social psychology of groups*. New York: Wiley, 1959.

29. Weiss, R. L. Contracts, cognition, and change: A behavioral approach to marriage therapy. *The Counseling Psychologist, 5*, 1975.

30. Wolpe, J. *The practice of behavior therapy*. New York: Pergamon Press, 1973.

Index of Types of Messages

About the Author

Joe Strayhorn, Jr. is currently an Associate in Psychiatry on the faculty of the Duke University Medical School where he teaches interviewing methods and marital and family therapy. He does clinical work with individuals, couples, and families. In connection with the Sociology and Psychiatry Mental Health Research Program at Duke, he is engaged in research on communication. He began using the methods and concepts described in this book for marital and family therapy, but has extended their use to a variety of other contexts, including group work, research, interview training, and prevention-oriented communication training for grade school students. He obtained a B.A. in Psychology at Amherst College, and an M.D. at Northwestern University. He completed residency training in Psychiatry at Duke University Medical Center.